Money, Wealth and Inequality - Book I
Economic History of Ancient India

Amrit Kumar

Table of contents

Dedication	1
Preface	3
1 Ancient Age	5

1.1 The Paleolithic Period – Humanity's Earliest Journey in India . . 5
    1.1.1 Introduction: Understanding Early Human Life Beyond Romance and Myth 5
    1.1.2 The Story Written in Stone: Paleolithic Tool Technologies 6
    1.1.3 Archaeological Evidence from Tamil Nadu: The Gateway to Understanding Indian Prehistory 7
    1.1.4 The Harsh Reality: What Paleolithic Life Actually Meant 8
    1.1.5 Paleolithic Economy and Subsistence: Constant Vigilance 10
1.2 The Neolithic Period – The First Agricultural Experiments . . . 11
    1.2.1 The Transition: From Wild to Domestic 11
    1.2.2 Technological Innovation: Polished Stone Tools 11
    1.2.3 Sanganakallu-Kupgal: The Neolithic Factory 12
    1.2.4 Pottery: From Hand-Made to Wheel-Thrown 13
    1.2.5 Agriculture and Animal Domestication: The Foundation of Settlement 14
    1.2.6 Settled Life: Permanence and Storage 15
    1.2.7 Burial Practices and Social Organization 16
    1.2.8 Specialized Occupations: Early Craft Production 16
1.3 The Copper Age: Transition and Technological Experimentation 17
    1.3.1 The Chalcolithic Period: Innovation and Regional Variation 17
    1.3.2 Northern India: The Age of Copper 18
    1.3.3 Southern India: Bypassing Copper for Iron 19
    1.3.4 The Gungeria Hoard: Bronze Age Metallurgy at Its Peak 19
    1.3.5 Symbolic Continuity: Coins and Sacred Symbols 20
1.4 The Indus Valley Civilization: Urban Achievement 21
    1.4.1 Urban Emergence: One of Three Great Bronze Age Civilizations 21
    1.4.2 Urban Planning and Architecture: The Grid City 22

	1.4.3	Sanitation Systems: Ahead of Their Time	23
	1.4.4	Material Culture and Daily Life	23
	1.4.5	Seals and the Undeciphered Script	24
	1.4.6	Metallurgy and Trade	25
1.5	Economic Development: The Evolution of Money		26
	1.5.1	Introduction: How Economies Functioned	26
	1.5.2	The Pastoral Stage: Cattle as Currency	27
	1.5.3	The Agricultural Stage: Commodity Money	28
	1.5.4	Legacy and Continuity	28
1.6	Conclusion: The Foundations of Civilization		29

2 Vedic Age 31

2.1	Introduction: The Transformation of Indian Civilization Through Vedic Times		31
2.2	The Early Rig Vedic Period: Pastoral Life and Tribal Society		32
	2.2.1	Introduction: Interpreting the Rigveda	32
	2.2.2	Geographic and Social Organization: The Punjab and Beyond	33
	2.2.3	The Pastoral Economy: Cattle and Wealth	33
	2.2.4	Animal Husbandry: Diversity Beyond Cattle	34
	2.2.5	Supplementary Agriculture: The Secondary Economy	35
	2.2.6	Craft Production and Occupational Specialization	36
	2.2.7	Trade and Exchange: Local Commerce and Long-Distance Networks	37
	2.2.8	Social Structure: The Emergence of Status Differentiation	38
	2.2.9	The Role of Women in Early Vedic Society	38
	2.2.10	Ritual and Religion: Sacrifice as the Center of Life	39
	2.2.11	The Role of Horses and Warfare	40
	2.2.12	Social Mobility and Merit in Early Vedic Society	41
2.3	The Later Vedic Period: Expansion, Urbanization, and Rigidification		42
	2.3.1	Introduction: The Changed World	42
	2.3.2	Geographic Expansion: From Punjab to the Gangetic Plains	43
	2.3.3	The Rise of Kingdoms: From Tribal Confederacies to Monarchical States	43
	2.3.4	Territorial Expansion and Ritual Legitimation of Power	44
	2.3.5	The Iron Age: Technology and Transformation	45
	2.3.6	Agriculture: Becoming the Dominant Subsistence Strategy	46
	2.3.7	Urbanization: The Emergence of Cities	47
	2.3.8	Trade and Commerce: Expanding Networks	47
	2.3.9	Occupational Specialization and the Crafts	48
	2.3.10	The Varna System: Codification of Social Hierarchy	49
	2.3.11	The Decline of Women's Status	50
	2.3.12	The Evolution of Religious Thought: Ritual and Philosophy	51
2.4	Economic Development: The Evolution of Monetary Systems		52
	2.4.1	From Cattle to Commodity Money	52
	2.4.2	The Significance of Monetary Evolution	53

TABLE OF CONTENTS

    2.5   Conclusion: Legacy and Transition 54

3 Age of Buddha   57
    3.1   Historical Context & Chronology 57
    3.2   The Mahajanapadas: Political Organization and Territorial States   58
           3.2.1   The Sixteen Great Kingdoms 58
           3.2.2   Monarchies and Republics: Two Paths of Organization . . 58
    3.3   Agricultural Economy and Rural Organization 59
           3.3.1   The Foundation: Agriculture and Village Life 59
           3.3.2   Village Organization and Social Hierarchy 60
           3.3.3   Taxation and Revenue: Formalization of State Extraction   61
    3.4   Trade, Commerce, and Market Development 62
           3.4.1   Domestic Trade and Market Networks 62
           3.4.2   Coinage and Monetary Evolution 62
           3.4.3   Long-Distance Trade Networks 63
    3.5   Urbanization: The Rise of Cities 64
           3.5.1   The Urban Wave 64
           3.5.2   Urban Occupations and Craft Specialization 65
           3.5.3   Urban Administration and Regulation 65
    3.6   Social Structure and the Varna System 66
           3.6.1   Occupational Specialization and Jati Formation 66
           3.6.2   The Varna System: Refinement During the Mahajanapada
                     Period 67
           3.6.3   Women and Social Status 68
    3.7   Administration and Governance 68
           3.7.1   The Monarchy: Centralized Authority 68
           3.7.2   Republican Governance: Assemblies and Collective Rule . 69
           3.7.3   Magadha: The Rising Power 70
    3.8   Occupations and Labor Organization 72
           3.8.1   The Jataka Tales as Economic Sources 72
           3.8.2   Agricultural and Animal Husbandry Occupations 72
           3.8.3   Craft and Manufacturing Occupations 73
           3.8.4   Trade and Commercial Occupations 73
           3.8.5   Labor and Servitude 74
    3.9   Currency and Monetary Systems 75
           3.9.1   Evolution from Commodity to Coined Money 75
           3.9.2   Regional Coin Types 75
           3.9.3   State Control and Standardization 76
    3.10 Credit, Lending, and Financial Instruments 77
           3.10.1 Emergence of Credit Systems 77
           3.10.2 Interest and Debt Relationships 77
           3.10.3 Guild Credit and Mutual Aid 78
    3.11 The Rise of Magadha and Political Consolidation 79
           3.11.1 Military and Administrative Innovations 79
           3.11.2 Strategic Expansion 80
           3.11.3 Intellectual and Spiritual Prestige 80

3.12 Conclusion: Transformation and Legacy 81

References **83**

About The Author **87**

Dedication

This book is dedicated to my mother and my greatest inspiration, Baidehi Kumari, whose values, wisdom, and rational way of living have shaped the person I am today. Her unwavering support, guidance, and faith in me have been my constant source of strength throughout my life.

Dedication

Preface

This book—Money, Wealth, and Inequality: Book I – Economic History of Ancient India—has been written with a single guiding purpose: to understand how the economic foundations of early Indian civilization shaped the enduring structures of wealth, inequality, technology, and social organization that continue to influence the subcontinent today.

For centuries, interpretations of ancient India have been dominated by mythology, romanticism, and fragmentary narratives that often obscure the material realities of life. This work seeks to bridge that gap by placing archaeological evidence, economic reasoning, and historical continuity at the center of analysis. The history of ancient India is not a tale of static perfection; it is a story of continuous innovation—beginning with the chipped stone tools of the Paleolithic age, advancing through the polished craftsmanship of the Neolithic, the metallurgical experiments of the Chalcolithic era, the urban sophistication of the Indus Valley Civilization, and the agrarian transformations of the Vedic and Brahmanical periods.

This volume is the first in a multi-part series examining how economic systems—tools, technology, trade, property relations, monetary forms, and institutional structures—evolved across millennia and shaped human life. The aim is not merely to catalogue historical facts, but to reconstruct how people lived, worked, produced, traded, governed, and conceptualized their world.

It is my hope that readers will find in these pages a clearer understanding of our economic past—not as a distant relic, but as a living foundation of the present. The same forces that shaped ancient societies continue to operate today: control over resources, technological change, organization of labour, and the persistent tension between wealth creation and social inequality.

May this book inspire curiosity about the long arc of Indian economic history and encourage deeper, evidence-based exploration of our shared past.

Amrit Kumar

Chapter 1

Ancient Age

1.1 The Paleolithic Period – Humanity's Earliest Journey in India

1.1.1 Introduction: Understanding Early Human Life Beyond Romance and Myth

For a long time, early human life has been imagined in romantic terms—as a simple and harmonious existence lived in close balance with nature. Archaeological research, however, offers a far more realistic and restrained picture. The earliest human communities in the Indian subcontinent lived under conditions that were demanding, uncertain, and often perilous. Survival was never guaranteed, and daily life revolved around responding to environmental pressures rather than enjoying any imagined primordial comfort. Excavations and material evidence make it clear that there was no "golden age" free from disease, injury, or death. Instead, what we observe is a slow and uneven process of adaptation shaped by climate fluctuations, changing landscapes, and limited technological means.

Paleolithic humans in India lived as hunter-gatherers, entirely dependent on naturally available resources. They had no knowledge of agriculture or animal domestication and relied on hunting wild game, fishing in rivers and streams, and collecting fruits, roots, tubers, and seeds. Food availability was unpredictable, and periods of relative abundance were frequently followed by scarcity. Mobility was therefore essential; groups moved from place to place in search of water, shelter, and food, leaving behind temporary camps rather than permanent settlements. The absence of pottery, architecture, or long-term storage further underlines the fragile nature of their subsistence.

Material culture during this period was limited but significant. Tools were fashioned primarily from stone, with occasional use of bone and wood, reflecting an early but growing understanding of raw materials and functionality. There is no evidence of land ownership, social stratification, or specialized occupations. Economic life was based on immediate needs rather than surplus or accumulation, and social organization was likely simple and flexible.

The Paleolithic period constitutes the longest phase of human history. Within this immense timeframe, the foundations of human behavior—tool-making, cooperation, environmental awareness, and adaptive intelligence—were laid. All later cultural and technological developments ultimately rest upon the slow but crucial achievements of this formative age, making the Paleolithic period indispensable to understanding the origins of human society in India.

1.1.2 The Story Written in Stone: Paleolithic Tool Technologies

Stone tools constitute the most enduring and informative evidence of Paleolithic life, serving as the primary means through which archaeologists reconstruct the technological and cognitive world of early humans. Unlike organic materials, stone survives across immense stretches of time, preserving clear traces of human intention, skill, and adaptation. The gradual transformation of stone tool technologies in India reflects not only improvements in craftsmanship but also deeper changes in planning ability, manual dexterity, and understanding of raw materials. Each technological stage marks a distinct phase in humanity's long engagement with its environment.

The Lower Paleolithic: Early Innovation

The Lower Paleolithic phase, represents the earliest sustained evidence of toolmaking in the Indian subcontinent. During this period, humans produced large, heavy-duty implements such as hand-axes, cleavers, and choppers. These tools, often associated with Acheulean traditions, were typically made from quartzite, a stone widely available in riverbeds and outcrops across peninsular India. Although simple in appearance, their manufacture required a clear understanding of how stone fractures under controlled blows.

Lower Paleolithic tools were multipurpose in nature. A single hand-axe could be used for cutting meat, breaking bones to extract marrow, processing plant matter, or scraping hides. The standardized shapes observed at several sites indicate that toolmakers followed mental templates, suggesting foresight and deliberate planning rather than random experimentation. These early innovations laid the foundation for all later technological developments.

The Middle Paleolithic: Technological Revolution

A major shift occurred during the Middle Paleolithic period. This phase is marked by the widespread adoption of prepared-core techniques, most notably the Levallois method. Unlike earlier approaches, this technique involved carefully shaping a stone core in advance so that a single, well-controlled strike would produce a flake of predetermined size and shape. The result was thinner, sharper, and more standardized tools, including scrapers, points, and cutting implements designed for specific functions.

The site of Attirampakkam in Tamil Nadu has fundamentally altered scholarly understanding of this transition in India. Excavations led by Kumar Akhilesh and Shanti Pappu have demonstrated that Levallois technology was present at the site as early as 385,000 years ago—far earlier than previously assumed. More than 7,000 tools recovered from the site indicate repeated and prolonged occupation, spanning nearly 200,000 years. This evidence challenges older models that viewed such technological sophistication as a late arrival from Africa, instead pointing to either early dispersals of advanced hominins or independent technological development within the subcontinent.

The Upper Paleolithic: Refinement and Specialization

The Upper Paleolithic period, represents the culmination of stone tool evolution in the prehistoric era. Toolmakers increasingly favored blade technology, producing long, narrow flakes with sharp, regular edges. Alongside these blades, microliths—small, finely made stone tools—became common. These were often hafted onto wooden or bone handles to create composite tools such as spears, arrows, and cutting instruments.

This emphasis on efficiency and specialization reflects a sophisticated understanding of material economy. By maximizing usable cutting edges from limited raw material, Upper Paleolithic communities demonstrated refined planning, adaptability, and technical skill. These developments not only enhanced hunting and processing activities but also paved the way for later innovations in subsistence and social organization, marking a crucial step toward the post-Paleolithic world.

1.1.3 Archaeological Evidence from Tamil Nadu: The Gateway to Understanding Indian Prehistory

Robert Bruce Foote's Pioneering Discovery

The formal study of Paleolithic archaeology in India began with an observation that would permanently alter perceptions of the subcontinent's human past. In 1863, Robert Bruce Foote, a British geologist working with the Geological Survey of India, was conducting fieldwork near Pallavaram, close to present-day Chennai. During this survey, he noticed several unusually shaped quartzite stones lying on the surface of a lateritic formation. Drawing upon his familiarity with European prehistoric discoveries—particularly the stone tools identified by Boucher de Perthes in France—Foote immediately recognized these objects as deliberately fashioned human implements rather than products of natural fracture.

On 30 May 1863, Foote formally recorded and collected a quartzite hand-axe, now acknowledged as the first scientifically documented Paleolithic tool from India. Its resemblance to Acheulean hand-axes from Europe demonstrated that early humans in India had followed similar technological principles, thereby challenging prevailing assumptions that prehistoric cultural development was largely confined to Europe. Initially, some scholars expressed skepticism, questioning whether such antiquity could truly be attributed to human activity in the Indian context. Foote's careful documentation and geological reasoning, however, gradually established the credibility of his claim.

Later the same year, Foote, along with his colleague William King, identified additional Paleolithic tools at Attirampakkam, further strengthening the case for an ancient human presence in southern India. Foote's commitment to scientific integrity was evident in his decision to preserve these artifacts in India rather than sell them to European collectors. His collection was ultimately housed in the Government Museum, Chennai, where it continues to serve as a cornerstone of Indian prehistoric studies.

Attirampakkam: A Record of Deep Time and Human Continuity

Attirampakkam, situated in the Kortallaiyar River basin northwest of Chennai, has since emerged as one of the most significant Paleolithic sites in the world. Archaeological research indicates that this location witnessed repeated human occupation over an exceptionally long duration, extending back nearly two million years. The site's stratified deposits preserve a continuous technological sequence, ranging from early Acheulean hand-axes and cleavers to Middle and Upper Paleolithic tool industries.

Systematic excavations conducted since the late twentieth century have produced tens of thousands of stone artifacts, enabling scholars to reconstruct a detailed technological and chronological framework. Advanced dating methods, particularly luminescence dating, have been crucial in establishing the antiquity of these layers and confirming the early emergence of sophisticated tool-making traditions at the site. Importantly, the archaeological record at Attirampakkam reflects not sporadic activity but repeated phases of settlement.

The enduring appeal of Attirampakkam to early humans can be attributed to favorable environmental conditions: access to perennial water sources, abundant quartzite suitable for tool production, and a landscape capable of supporting hunting and gathering activities. Together, these features made the site a stable focal point for human life across vast stretches of prehistory, offering an unparalleled window into the deep antiquity of human adaptation and technological evolution in the Indian subcontinent.

1.1.4 The Harsh Reality: What Paleolithic Life Actually Meant

Stone tools reveal how Paleolithic people worked, but the physical remains of human bodies reveal how they lived—and how they died. Skeletal and dental evidence recovered from Paleolithic contexts across the world, including material relevant to South Asia, paints a stark picture of existence marked by constant

1.1. THE PALEOLITHIC PERIOD – HUMANITY'S EARLIEST JOURNEY IN INDIA 9

physical stress, disease, and danger. Far from being a life of ease or harmony, Paleolithic survival demanded resilience in the face of persistent biological and environmental threats.

Mortality and Life Expectancy

Studies of Paleolithic skeletal populations indicate an extremely high mortality rate. Life expectancy at birth is estimated to have been no more than 25–30 years, with a large proportion of individuals dying well before reaching middle age. This pattern was not simply the result of infant mortality, although childhood deaths were common. Even among those who survived early childhood, the likelihood of reaching old age was very low. Young adults frequently succumbed to disease, injury, or nutritional stress, keeping average life spans consistently short.

Infectious disease appears to have been the single most significant cause of death. Without any understanding of pathogens, sanitation, or medical treatment, Paleolithic populations were highly vulnerable to parasitic infections, gastrointestinal illnesses leading to dehydration, and respiratory diseases. Injuries that are easily survivable today—infected wounds, minor fractures, or fever—could rapidly become fatal. Seasonal food shortages further compounded these risks. Periods of starvation or chronic malnutrition weakened immune systems, making individuals even more susceptible to disease.

Violence also formed a measurable component of mortality. Skeletal evidence suggests that a notable proportion of deaths—estimated at around 15 percent— were related to interpersonal or inter-group conflict. Competition over food resources, territory, or social tensions within small groups likely contributed to this pattern, reflecting the fragile balance under which Paleolithic communities operated.

Physical Stress and Hardship

The human skeleton itself preserves long-term records of hardship. Many Paleolithic individuals exhibit dental enamel hypoplasia—lines or pits on teeth caused by severe physiological stress during childhood, such as prolonged hunger or serious illness. Because tooth enamel does not regenerate, these defects permanently recorded episodes of deprivation experienced early in life. Their prevalence indicates that nutritional stress was not exceptional but routine.

Skeletal remains also frequently show healed fractures, joint degeneration, and trauma-related injuries. Broken limbs, damaged vertebrae, and cranial injuries attest to the dangers of hunting large animals, accidents during daily activities, and episodes of violence. Importantly, the presence of healed injuries carries an important social implication. Survival after serious trauma would have been impossible without assistance. This suggests that Paleolithic groups practiced care for injured or incapacitated members, pointing to strong social bonds and cooperative behavior even under extreme conditions.

Taken together, the biological evidence underscores a central reality of Paleolithic life: it was harsh, uncertain, and physically taxing. Yet within these constraints, early humans displayed resilience, cooperation, and an ability to endure conditions that would challenge modern populations. Their survival, against overwhelming odds, laid the biological and social foundations for all later human societies.

1.1.5 Paleolithic Economy and Subsistence: Constant Vigilance

The subsistence system of Paleolithic communities was entirely dependent on the exploitation of wild resources. In this sense, the term "economy" can only be used in a very limited way, as there was no production of food, storage of surplus, or long-term planning beyond immediate survival. Daily life was organized around securing enough food to sustain the group, a task that required continuous effort, mobility, and alertness to changing environmental conditions.

Hunting occupied a central place in Paleolithic subsistence, though it was neither reliable nor consistently successful. Archaeological and faunal evidence indicates that people pursued large and medium-sized animals such as wild cattle (aurochs), deer, wild boar, and smaller mammals using spears, clubs, and simple hunting strategies. These weapons demanded close-range engagement and exposed hunters to significant risk of injury or death. A failed hunt could mean hunger for the entire group, underscoring the precarious nature of meat acquisition. Fishing in rivers and streams provided an important supplementary source of protein, particularly during periods when terrestrial game was scarce or seasonally unavailable.

Plant gathering, largely carried out by women and children, likely formed the most stable component of the Paleolithic diet. Wild roots, tubers, fruits, berries, nuts, and edible leaves supplied essential calories and nutrients, even though such foods are underrepresented in the archaeological record due to their poor preservation. Ethnographic parallels and botanical studies strongly suggest that plant foods contributed a substantial share of daily energy intake, despite the common emphasis on hunting in popular narratives.

Survival under these conditions required an intimate and detailed knowledge of the natural environment. Paleolithic groups possessed a deep understanding of seasonal cycles, animal behavior, and plant growth patterns. They knew where animals migrated, when certain plants ripened, and which landscapes offered reliable water sources. This environmental knowledge was cumulative, passed down through generations through observation and experience. Nevertheless, uncertainty remained unavoidable. Climatic variation, droughts, or shifts in animal movement could quickly disrupt subsistence patterns. Constant vigilance and adaptability were therefore not optional but fundamental to Paleolithic life, shaping both daily routines and long-term survival strategies.

1.2 The Neolithic Period – The First Agricultural Experiments

1.2.1 The Transition: From Wild to Domestic

Human communities in different parts of the world—including the Indian subcontinent—began to undergo a gradual yet transformative shift in the way they secured their food. This long and uneven process, conventionally described as the Neolithic transition, marked the first sustained attempts to cultivate plants and manage animal populations rather than relying exclusively on wild resources. Archaeological and cultural studies indicate that this change did not occur as a sudden "revolution" but unfolded slowly, through repeated experimentation, local adaptation, and incremental learning spread across many generations.

In India, the move toward agriculture emerged through regional trajectories rather than a single uniform pattern. Early communities began to observe plant growth cycles, selectively gather preferred species, and eventually protect or replant useful plants near their settlements. At the same time, certain animals that had previously been hunted began to be managed, protected, and gradually domesticated. These early practices did not immediately replace hunting and gathering. Instead, for long periods, farming and foraging existed side by side, creating mixed subsistence systems in which cultivated foods supplemented wild resources.

The pace of this transformation varied considerably from region to region. In some areas, environmental conditions favored relatively rapid adoption of cultivation, while in others the shift was extremely slow, extending over centuries. This prolonged overlap suggests that early farming was initially risky and uncertain, and communities were reluctant to abandon proven hunting-gathering strategies until agricultural practices demonstrated greater reliability. Over time, however, the cumulative benefits of controlled food production—greater predictability, increased population support, and the possibility of more permanent settlements—gradually reshaped social organization and daily life.

This transitional phase represents one of the most consequential turning points in human history. It laid the foundations for settled village life, new forms of property relations, and eventually the complex economic and social systems that would characterize later periods of Indian history.

1.2.2 Technological Innovation: Polished Stone Tools

One of the most distinctive technological developments of the Neolithic period was the introduction of polished stone tools. Unlike Paleolithic implements, which were shaped primarily by striking stone against stone, Neolithic tools were carefully ground and polished to produce smooth surfaces and finely sharpened edges. This method required considerably more time and labor, but it yielded stronger, more durable, and more efficient implements, particularly suited to the demands of an increasingly settled and agricultural way of life.

Polished stone axes and adzes formed the core of this new toolkit. These tools were especially effective for woodworking, allowing people to fell trees, shape timber, and clear forested land for cultivation. The shift toward farming made such activities essential. Forest clearance was necessary to create arable fields, while the construction of houses, fences, storage structures, and simple furniture required a steady supply of worked wood. Polished tools, with their sharper and more resilient cutting edges, made these tasks faster and more reliable than earlier flaked implements.

Archaeological excavations across Neolithic sites in India reveal a diverse and functionally specialized toolkit. Alongside axes and adzes, researchers have identified chisels and gouges used for shaping wood and bone, grinding stones and corn-crushers for processing cultivated grains, scrapers for hide working, and picks for digging activities. Perforated stones, often interpreted as weights attached to digging sticks, suggest the development of simple agricultural implements used in planting and soil preparation.

The variety and specialization of these tools reflect a significant change in daily life. Neolithic communities were no longer organized solely around immediate subsistence needs but were engaged in a broader range of productive activities—cultivation, construction, storage, and craftwork. Polished stone technology therefore represents more than a technical improvement; it marks a fundamental shift toward a more complex, settled, and materially intensive form of life that laid the groundwork for later village economies.

1.2.3 Sanganakallu-Kupgal: The Neolithic Factory

The Neolithic site of Sanganakallu–Kupgal, situated near Bellary in eastern Karnataka, provides one of the clearest windows into large-scale and organized tool production in prehistoric India. First brought to scholarly attention through excavations conducted by B. Subbarao in 1946, the site has since been the subject of systematic archaeological investigation, particularly from 1997 onward. These studies reveal that Sanganakallu–Kupgal was not merely a habitation area but a highly specialized center of stone-tool manufacture operating on a remarkable scale.

The physical landscape of the site played a decisive role in its development. A prominent dyke of dolerite—a dense and durable volcanic stone—runs through the surrounding granite hill complex, measuring roughly 10 to 30 meters in width. Neolithic communities quickly recognized the superior quality of this stone for tool production, especially for polished axes and adzes. As a result, quarrying and manufacturing activities became concentrated around this natural resource, giving rise to an extensive production zone supported by at least three substantial hilltop settlements.

Archaeological excavations have yielded tens of thousands of stone flakes, rough blanks, partially finished implements, and completed tools. This enormous volume of material clearly reflects systematic and sustained manufacturing rather than casual, household-level production. Detailed analysis shows that tool making followed a structured sequence of stages, from quarrying and initial flaking to careful grinding and polishing. Importantly, the variability in workmanship suggests a division of labor: some individuals specialized in extracting raw material and rough shaping, while others, likely more skilled artisans, focused on finishing and polishing the tools to their final form.

This organized production implies important social and economic developments. The presence of specialized craftspeople indicates that not all members of the community were directly engaged in food production. Such specialization presupposes the existence of surplus resources and some form of exchange mechanism through which finished tools could be traded for food and other necessities. Sanganakallu–Kupgal therefore represents an early example of craft specialization and proto-industrial organization in Neolithic India, marking a significant step toward more complex economic systems in later periods.

1.2.4 Pottery: From Hand-Made to Wheel-Thrown

Pottery represents one of the most visible material markers of Neolithic life in India, yet archaeological evidence shows that it did not appear at the very beginning of the agricultural transition. Early farming communities initially managed without ceramic containers, relying instead on baskets, gourds, wooden vessels, and skins. Pottery became common only after village life had become more firmly established, when the need for durable storage, cooking, and transport containers grew more pressing.

The earliest pottery was handmade and produced through the coiling technique. Potters shaped long rolls of clay and built vessels by layering these coils upward, carefully smoothing and joining them to form continuous walls. These early vessels were generally utilitarian, made from coarse clay and fired at relatively low temperatures. Their appearance was simple—often dull brown, black, or grey—reflecting an emphasis on functionality rather than decoration.

Over time, significant technological refinement took place. The introduction of the potter's wheel—initially in the form of a slow wheel or tournette—marked a turning point in ceramic production. As wheel technology improved, faster rotation allowed the development of true wheel-throwing techniques. Potters could now produce vessels with thinner, more uniform walls, improved structural strength, and more standardized shapes. This not only enhanced the efficiency of production but also increased the range and quality of ceramic forms available to Neolithic communities.

Regional variation soon became a defining feature of Indian Neolithic pottery. Archaeological evidence points to the emergence of distinct ceramic traditions, including plain wares in some areas, red and grey wares in others, as well as ochre-colored pottery in specific zones. In southern India, the appearance of black-

and-red ware marked another important stage in ceramic development. These regional styles reflect local preferences, raw material availability, and evolving cultural identities, underscoring the growing complexity and diversification of Neolithic material culture.

1.2.5 Agriculture and Animal Domestication: The Foundation of Settlement

The establishment of permanent or semi-permanent settlements in Neolithic India was made possible by a gradual but decisive shift from exclusive reliance on wild resources to the deliberate management of plants and animals. This transformation did not unfold uniformly across the subcontinent. Instead, different regions followed distinct trajectories in which herding and cultivation developed at varying speeds and often in different sequences, reflecting local environmental and cultural conditions.

Animal Domestication: Earlier Than Agriculture

Archaeological evidence suggests that the management of animals began before systematic crop cultivation in several parts of the northwestern subcontinent. The site of Mehrgarh, located in the Kachi plains, provides the clearest early evidence of this process. In its earliest Neolithic levels, remains of domesticated sheep and goats appear alongside bones of wild animals, indicating a mixed subsistence economy that combined hunting with early pastoral practices. Over time, the proportion of domesticated animal remains steadily increased, while those of wild species declined, pointing to a gradual intensification of herding.

By later phases of occupation, cattle—particularly the humped Bos indicus, well adapted to subtropical environments—had also been domesticated at Mehrgarh. These developments reflect a long-term process rather than a sudden innovation. Through generations of close contact, selective hunting, protection, and breeding, human communities gradually shaped animal populations to favor docility, manageable size, and other desirable traits, eventually giving rise to fully domesticated herds.

Domesticated animals provided more than meat. Cattle offered milk and dairy products, sheep and goats supplied wool, and oxen became crucial sources of traction for transport and ploughing. This range of "secondary products" transformed herding into a sophisticated economic strategy, supporting food security, mobility, and early agricultural activity.

Plant Cultivation: Regional Diversity

Plant domestication in Neolithic India followed regionally distinct patterns. In the northwestern regions, including parts of present-day Pakistan and northern India, early cultivation focused on crops such as wheat, barley, lentils, and peas. At Mehrgarh, the gradual appearance of carbonized seeds, grinding stones, and storage pits documents the slow incorporation of farming into daily life and the growing importance of cereal cultivation alongside animal husbandry.

In contrast, southern India developed an independent agricultural tradition centered on millets. Archaeological evidence from Neolithic sites across the peninsula indicates that browntop millet served as the primary staple grain of early farming communities. Over time, other millets such as pearl millet and sorghum became increasingly significant, the latter likely introduced through wider contacts beyond the subcontinent. Excavations at Sanganakallu–Kupgal and related sites show that early southern Neolithic settlements relied heavily on pastoralism and hunting, with cultivation emerging gradually and, in some areas, never fully replacing older subsistence practices.

Together, these developments in animal domestication and plant cultivation laid the economic foundation for more stable settlements, population growth, and the emergence of increasingly complex social structures in Neolithic India.

1.2.6 Settled Life: Permanence and Storage

The adoption of agriculture brought about a decisive transformation in patterns of residence and daily life. Unlike Paleolithic hunter-gatherers, who moved seasonally in response to shifting availability of wild resources, Neolithic communities were increasingly tied to specific locations. Cultivated fields required continuous attention—sowing, weeding, harvesting, and protecting crops—making prolonged or permanent settlement not only possible but necessary.

Archaeological evidence from Neolithic sites across the Indian subcontinent reveals the emergence of more durable domestic architecture. Houses were commonly built in circular or rectangular forms using mud, reeds, and thatch, materials readily available in the surrounding environment. These structures were clearly intended for long-term occupation. Within them, excavations have identified cooking hearths, grinding stones for processing cereals, and fixed installations associated with daily household activities. Such features distinguish Neolithic dwellings sharply from the temporary camps characteristic of mobile foraging communities.

Perhaps the most significant material expression of settled life is the appearance of storage facilities. Granaries, underground storage pits, and ceramic containers indicate that Neolithic households were able to preserve surplus produce from successful harvests. This marked a fundamental change in attitudes toward food. Instead of consuming resources as they were acquired, communities could now plan for the future, storing grain and other produce for periods of scarcity.

The ability to accumulate and manage surplus had far-reaching social consequences. Stored food provided greater security against famine and seasonal shortfalls, supporting larger and more stable populations. It also made possible the emergence of occupational specialization, as some individuals could devote themselves to crafts or other activities rather than direct food production. Over time, control over stored resources contributed to differences in wealth and influence within communities, laying the groundwork for social differentiation and more complex forms of organization that would characterize later phases of Indian prehistory.

1.2.7 Burial Practices and Social Organization

Neolithic burial evidence provides a valuable perspective on social structure, belief systems, and concepts of status within early settled communities. One of the most significant burial complexes in southern India is located at Adichanallur, in the Tamirabharani River valley of Tamil Nadu. Excavations conducted since the nineteenth century have brought to light a large cemetery comprising more than 160 urn burials. In these burials, human remains were carefully placed in large ceramic vessels, typically in a crouched posture, a funerary practice that became characteristic of southern Indian Neolithic and early protohistoric traditions.

The Adichanallur burials are notable for the richness and variety of grave goods deposited alongside the deceased. Archaeological investigations have recorded pottery vessels, metal implements, ornaments, and personal objects placed within or near the burial urns. Among these finds are iron tools, bronze artifacts, gold diadems and jewelry, and beads fashioned from shell and stone. In several burials, traces of stored grain and millet have also been identified, suggesting that food offerings formed part of mortuary ritual.

The uneven distribution of grave goods across the cemetery points to emerging social differentiation. While all individuals were accorded formal burial and associated offerings, some graves contained far more elaborate and valuable assemblages than others. This pattern implies differences in social status, family prestige, or accumulated wealth within the community. Such variation reflects a society that had moved beyond egalitarian organization toward more stratified forms of social structure.

The care invested in constructing ceramic urns, arranging the bodies, and placing goods with the deceased also reveals shared beliefs concerning death and continuity beyond life. These practices suggest that Neolithic communities at Adichanallur viewed burial not merely as disposal of the dead but as a meaningful ritual act, reinforcing social identity, memory, and collective values within early settled society.

1.2.8 Specialized Occupations: Early Craft Production

By the later phases of the Neolithic period, subsistence activities were increasingly complemented by specialized crafts that went beyond basic food production. Among the most significant of these emerging occupations were mining and early metallurgical practices, which point to growing technical knowledge, organized labor, and participation in wider exchange networks. These developments signal an important stage in the diversification of economic life in prehistoric India.

Gold Mining at Maski

The site of Maski, located in the Raichur district of Karnataka, provides some of the earliest and most compelling evidence for organized gold mining in the Indian subcontinent. Archaeological and historical analyses indicate that communities in this region were among the first in India to recognize, extract, and utilize gold-bearing ores. Trace element studies conducted on gold artifacts recovered from Indus Valley Civilization sites have revealed chemical signatures consistent with Maski gold, suggesting that precious metal from this region entered long-distance trade networks and was transported northward to major urban centers of the Indus system.

The mining operations associated with Maski reflect a high level of technical understanding. Ancient miners were able to identify auriferous rock formations, extract ore through labor-intensive quarrying, and separate gold from surrounding material. The region also contains some of India's deepest ancient gold mines, many of which date to the mid–first millennium BCE. Although these deeper mines belong to a later chronological phase, they represent the continuation and intensification of mining traditions that appear to have had much earlier roots in the region.

The existence of such organized extraction and the movement of gold across considerable distances imply both surplus production and structured systems of exchange. Mining at Maski therefore illustrates the emergence of specialized occupational roles and the integration of Neolithic and early protohistoric communities into broader economic networks, foreshadowing the complex craft industries and long-distance trade that would characterize later periods of Indian history.

1.3 The Copper Age: Transition and Technological Experimentation

1.3.1 The Chalcolithic Period: Innovation and Regional Variation

Many regions of the Indian subcontinent experienced a transitional cultural phase known as the Chalcolithic or Copper Age. The term "Chalcolithic," derived from the Greek words chalkos (copper) and lithos (stone), reflects the defining technological characteristic of this period: the coexistence of metal and stone tools within the same communities. Copper implements began to appear for the first time, yet they did not immediately replace established stone technologies. Instead, both materials were used side by side, indicating a gradual and experimental process of technological adoption rather than a sudden replacement of older traditions.

This phase was marked by pronounced regional diversity. Archaeological evidence shows that different parts of the subcontinent adopted copper technology at different times and to varying degrees. In some areas, copper objects remained relatively rare and largely ceremonial, while in others they became more integrated into everyday economic life. Such variation reflects differences in access to metal-bearing ores, local technological traditions, patterns of interregional contact, and environmental conditions that shaped subsistence strategies and craft production.

The Chalcolithic period also coincided with broader changes in settlement patterns, craft specialization, and exchange networks. As communities became increasingly sedentary and surplus production expanded, there was greater scope for experimentation with new materials and techniques. Copper tools—although initially limited in number—represented a significant conceptual shift, introducing metallurgy as a new domain of knowledge and laying the technological foundations for the more widespread use of metals in subsequent periods.

Thus, the Chalcolithic phase stands as a formative bridge between the Neolithic world of polished stone tools and the later fully developed metal-using cultures, highlighting both continuity and innovation within prehistoric Indian society.

1.3.2 Northern India: The Age of Copper

In northern India, particularly within the Gangetic valley and its adjoining regions, a distinctive phase often referred to as the "Copper Age" developed between the Neolithic and the Iron Age. This phase is most clearly represented by the phenomenon of copper hoards. These hoards consist of large, deliberately buried collections of copper implements, and they provide some of the earliest and most substantial evidence for organized copper metallurgy in the region.

The objects recovered from these hoards display a remarkable range of forms. Archaeologists have identified axes, celts, harpoons, spears, swords, anthropomorphic figures, and other specialized implements. The technical quality of these objects suggests a well-developed knowledge of smelting, casting, and shaping copper, indicating that metallurgy had become an established craft rather than an occasional experiment. The sheer quantity of metal present in many hoards also implies access to ore sources, skilled artisans, and networks for the distribution of finished products.

The practice of burying copper objects in large groups rather than dispersing them through everyday use raises important interpretive questions. Scholars have proposed several explanations. Some view the hoards as emergency caches hidden during times of conflict or social instability. Others suggest that they represent accumulated wealth buried for safekeeping, possibly intended to be retrieved later. A further interpretation sees them as ritual deposits, deliberately placed in the ground as offerings or symbolic acts rather than as utilitarian stores.

Regardless of the precise motivation behind their deposition, the copper hoards of northern India demonstrate that copper working had reached a considerable

1.3. THE COPPER AGE: TRANSITION AND TECHNOLOGICAL EXPERIMENTATION

scale and level of sophistication. They mark a critical stage in the technological and social evolution of the region, bridging earlier stone-based traditions and the later widespread adoption of iron technology.

1.3.3 Southern India: Bypassing Copper for Iron

One of the most striking regional contrasts in Indian prehistory is seen in southern India, where archaeological evidence points to a markedly different technological trajectory from that of the northern plains. Unlike the Gangetic and northwestern regions, which experienced a prolonged Chalcolithic or Copper Age, southern India shows little evidence for a comparable phase of copper or bronze tool use. Excavations of Neolithic and early Iron Age sites in the Deccan and adjoining areas have yielded very few copper implements, and those that do appear are rare and isolated rather than forming a coherent technological tradition.

Instead, the material record suggests that communities in southern India moved almost directly from stone tool technologies to the widespread adoption of iron. Polished stone axes, adzes, and other Neolithic implements continued in use until they were gradually replaced by iron tools, without an intervening period in which copper or bronze played a dominant role. This direct transition represents a significant technological divergence within the subcontinent.

Such a pattern reflects differing regional histories of contact, resource availability, and innovation. Access to copper ores, established metallurgical traditions, and trade connections may have been more limited in the southern peninsula than in northern regions, reducing the incentive or opportunity to adopt copper technology. At the same time, once iron-working knowledge became available, it appears to have been rapidly integrated into local economies, perhaps because iron tools offered clear functional advantages for agriculture and woodworking.

The southern Indian sequence therefore highlights the diversity of technological pathways within prehistoric India. Rather than following a single, uniform progression from stone to copper to iron, different regions adopted new materials in ways shaped by local environmental conditions, cultural networks, and practical needs.

1.3.4 The Gungeria Hoard: Bronze Age Metallurgy at Its Peak

Among the archaeological discoveries associated with India's Copper Age, the Gungeria hoard stands out for both its scale and its technological significance. The hoard was accidentally discovered in 1870 in the Balaghat district of Madhya Pradesh when a farmer, while ploughing his field, struck a buried cache of metal objects. Subsequent excavation under the supervision of Deputy Commissioner Bloomfield revealed an extraordinary assemblage consisting of 424 copper implements and 102 thin silver plates, buried at a depth of about three feet. The total weight of the copper objects alone amounted to approximately 376–377 kilograms, while the silver pieces together weighed close to 966 grams.

The composition and manufacture of the Gungeria implements demonstrate a remarkably advanced level of metallurgical expertise. Scientific examination shows that the copper used was of very high purity, containing only about 0.5 percent lead—comparable to what is known as "blister copper," an intermediate but refined stage in modern copper production. Achieving such purity would have required a sequence of technically demanding processes, including careful selection and preparation of ore, roasting to modify its chemical composition, fluxing to reduce melting temperatures, smelting with charcoal to extract metallic copper, and subsequent refining to remove remaining impurities. Each of these steps presupposes specialized knowledge and skilled workmanship.

Contemporary scholars of the nineteenth century described the Gungeria hoard as "the most important discovery of instruments of copper yet recorded in the Old World," reflecting the unprecedented quantity and quality of the material recovered. The assemblage includes a wide variety of celts (axes), weapons, and utilitarian tools, indicating that the hoard was not the product of a single artisan but rather the accumulated output of a broader community or region over time. Its composition suggests that the objects may have represented stored wealth, trade commodities, or ceremonial deposits, underscoring the economic and social importance of metallurgy during India's Copper Age.

1.3.5 Symbolic Continuity: Coins and Sacred Symbols

Archaeological evidence suggests that technological change in ancient India did not sever ties with older systems of meaning and belief. Instead, many symbolic traditions that had developed in prehistoric contexts continued to exert influence well into the early historical period. A particularly striking example of this continuity is provided by punch-marked coins, the earliest known form of Indian coinage. These coins, made of copper or silver, were produced by striking a series of small symbols onto blank metal pieces rather than casting or engraving complete designs.

The symbols impressed on punch-marked coins reveal deep connections with much older cultural imagery. They include representations of animals long familiar in Indian symbolic tradition—bulls, oxen, zebu cattle, elephants, tigers, and rhinoceroses. Alongside these appear geometric and auspicious motifs such as the swastika, the Ujjain symbol, wheels, conch shells, and lotus flowers, as well as depictions of natural elements like the sun, moon, hills, trees, and water sources. Many of these motifs can be traced conceptually to prehistoric visual traditions, where animals and natural forces held strong symbolic significance in ritual and social life.

The discovery of punch-marked coins in association with Pandukulis—megalithic burial structures characteristic of southern India—further underlines this continuity. Their presence within such funerary contexts indicates that these coins were already in circulation during the Iron Age–Early Historical phase, a time of expanding trade networks and emerging political structures. Yet even within these new economic systems, older symbolic vocabularies were retained.

This persistence of imagery suggests that cultural change in ancient India was cumulative rather than disruptive. Symbols such as the swastika, the zebu bull, and the lotus did not disappear with the advent of metallurgy or coinage. Instead, they were absorbed into new material forms and economic practices, allowing prehistoric symbolic traditions to remain active components of religious belief, social identity, and political expression in the historical period.

1.4 The Indus Valley Civilization: Urban Achievement

1.4.1 Urban Emergence: One of Three Great Bronze Age Civilizations

The northwestern regions of the Indian subcontinent witnessed the rise of one of the world's earliest and most accomplished urban cultures—the Indus Valley Civilization. Centered in the valleys of the Indus River and its tributaries, this civilization developed in broad chronological parallel with ancient Egypt and Mesopotamia, forming the third great urban tradition of the Bronze Age world. By its mature phase, the Indus realm extended across a vast geographic area and supported a population estimated between four and six million people, living in more than a thousand towns, cities, and rural settlements.

The scale and organization of this civilization were extraordinary. Sites such as Harappa, Mohenjo-daro, Dholavira, and numerous smaller settlements reveal a remarkable degree of standardization in bricks, weights, measures, and urban layouts, indicating coordinated planning across large distances. This level of uniformity suggests not only shared technical knowledge but also strong systems of communication and regulation that bound the settlements into a coherent cultural and economic network.

What makes the Indus Valley Civilization particularly distinctive is its apparent social and political character. Unlike Egypt, with its monumental pyramids and divine kingship, or Mesopotamia, with its imposing temples and royal palaces, Indus cities lack clear evidence of grandiose royal residences or centralized religious complexes. Instead, urban space appears to have been organized around residential neighborhoods, civic infrastructure, and communal facilities. This pattern has led many scholars to suggest that Indus society may have been comparatively egalitarian, or at least less overtly hierarchical, than its contemporaries.

Despite the absence of ostentatious monuments, the Indus civilization achieved an exceptional level of urban sophistication. Carefully planned street grids, standardized construction materials, and highly developed civic amenities reflect an advanced understanding of urban management. These achievements demonstrate that complex urban life could flourish without relying on the highly centralized and visibly hierarchical political structures that characterized other early civilizations.

1.4.2 Urban Planning and Architecture: The Grid City

The principal cities of the Indus Valley Civilization, most notably Harappa in Punjab and Mohenjo-daro in Sindh, present one of the clearest early examples of deliberate urban planning in the ancient world. Excavations at these sites reveal that streets were laid out according to a precise orthogonal grid. Broad main avenues, aligned closely with the cardinal directions, measured roughly 7.2 meters in width, while narrower secondary lanes averaged about 1.8 meters. This regular street pattern divided the cities into well-defined blocks that accommodated residential quarters, workshops, and civic spaces, indicating that the urban layout was conceived in advance rather than shaped by unplanned growth.

A striking feature of Indus architecture is the extraordinary degree of standardization. Throughout the cities, bricks were manufactured to uniform proportions, typically following a 1:2:4 ratio, with common dimensions around $7 \times 14 \times 28$ centimeters. The consistent use of these standardized bricks across vast distances implies strong technical coordination and shared construction norms, if not centralized oversight of brick production. Such uniformity reflects a high level of social organization and a collective commitment to planned urban development.

Buildings were predominantly constructed of baked brick, chosen for its durability and resistance to moisture. Houses generally featured thick walls and internal courtyards, around which rooms were arranged. These courtyards provided light, ventilation, and multipurpose working areas, making them well suited to the region's warm climate. The consistent architectural style across neighborhoods suggests that even domestic structures adhered to broader planning principles.

The most iconic monument of Mohenjo-daro is the Great Bath, which exemplifies the civilization's advanced engineering capabilities. Measuring approximately 12 meters from north to south and 7 meters from east to west, with a depth of about 2.4 meters, the bath was carefully constructed to be watertight. Its floor comprised two layers of brick laid in gypsum mortar, with a layer of bitumen sealed between them to prevent seepage. Water was supplied by a large adjacent well, while used water was drained through corbelled channels that carried wastewater away from the structure. These features demonstrate a sophisticated understanding of hydraulic engineering and public infrastructure within Indus urban centers.

1.4.3 Sanitation Systems: Ahead of Their Time

Among the most technically impressive achievements of the Indus Valley Civilization were its highly developed systems for drainage and sanitation. These were not incidental additions to urban life but integral components of city planning. Archaeological evidence shows that individual houses commonly contained private bathing areas and latrines, indicating that sanitation was treated as a domestic necessity rather than a communal afterthought.

Wastewater was carefully managed through a network of drains and channels. Within houses, used water was directed into covered drains that ran beneath or alongside the streets. These household drains connected to larger brick-lined street channels that extended along both sides of major thoroughfares. From there, wastewater flowed into main sewer lines that conveyed it toward collection points or out of the city limits altogether. The presence of inspection holes placed at regular intervals demonstrates that these systems were designed for cleaning and maintenance, reflecting a conscious concern for long-term functionality.

In addition to linear drains, rectangular sump pits were installed at strategic points within the urban layout. These pits were designed to trap solid waste before wastewater entered the main drainage system, preventing blockages and improving overall sanitation. The systematic placement of these features throughout Indus cities indicates a comprehensive and citywide approach to waste management rather than isolated or ad hoc solutions.

Such an integrated sanitation infrastructure was unparalleled in the ancient world and would not be matched in complexity for millennia. It reveals a sophisticated understanding of public health and environmental hygiene. The prevalence of bathing platforms and multiple washing areas within houses further suggests that regular bathing held both practical and ritual importance. This emphasis on cleanliness and purification anticipates later Indian cultural traditions in which water and bathing occupy a central symbolic and religious role.

1.4.4 Material Culture and Daily Life

Excavations at Indus Valley sites provide a rich and intimate picture of everyday life within one of the world's earliest urban societies. The material remains recovered from cities such as Harappa and Mohenjo-daro reveal communities that were not only technologically accomplished but also culturally expressive and socially active.

Pottery formed an essential part of domestic life and displays considerable diversity in both technique and decoration. Archaeological assemblages include hand-made as well as wheel-thrown vessels, indicating continuity with earlier ceramic traditions alongside more refined production methods. Many vessels were plain and utilitarian, designed for cooking, storage, and transport, while others were decorated with black-painted motifs, geometric designs, or incised patterns. Rare polychrome wares—painted in multiple colors—suggest objects reserved for special, possibly ceremonial or high-status contexts, pointing to differentiation in social use and function.

Terracotta figurines provide particularly evocative insights into Indus artistic and cultural values. Numerous miniature animal figures, toy carts complete with wheels, and small human figurines have been recovered, indicating both artistic creativity and the presence of children's toys. Among the most celebrated finds is the bronze "Dancing Girl" of Mohenjo-daro. Though only about 10 centimeters tall, the figure conveys a striking sense of movement and confidence. Her posture and adornment—particularly the stack of bangles on her arms—suggest that bracelets made of shell, terracotta, faience, and metal were common elements of dress, especially among women.

Recreation also formed part of urban life. Six-sided dice marked with dotted faces, closely resembling modern dice, have been discovered at several Indus sites. Variations in their markings imply either imperfect standardization or intentional stylistic differences. Their presence demonstrates that games involving chance and structured rules were known and enjoyed, adding another dimension to our understanding of social interaction and leisure within Indus civilization.

Together, these material remains portray a society that balanced practical domestic needs with artistic expression, social leisure, and cultural continuity, underscoring the human richness of Indus urban life.

1.4.5 Seals and the Undeciphered Script

Among the most distinctive and intellectually challenging artifacts of the Indus Valley Civilization are the thousands of inscribed seals recovered from major urban centers and smaller settlements alike. Approximately 4,000 such seals are known, most commonly made of steatite, a soft stone well suited to fine carving and mass production. Typically square or rectangular in form, these seals were carved in intaglio, so that when pressed onto clay or other soft material they produced raised impressions. The reverse side usually bears a boss or loop, allowing the seal to be suspended from a cord and worn as a personal emblem or carried for official use.

The imagery engraved on these seals displays a striking consistency, pointing to shared cultural and symbolic conventions across the Indus world. The most frequently depicted figure is the so-called "unicorn," a single-horned animal that does not correspond to any known species, suggesting a mythic or ritual significance. Other common motifs include humped zebu cattle, bulls, elephants, tigers, rhinoceroses, and fish. Some seals even show composite creatures formed by combining features of different animals, indicating a symbolic vocabulary that remains poorly understood but was clearly meaningful within Indus society.

Almost all seals bear short inscriptions, usually consisting of five or six characters, though a few contain much longer sequences of up to 26 symbols. The Indus script remains undeciphered, despite more than a century of scholarly effort. It is estimated to include between 400 and 600 distinct signs, placing it among the more complex early writing systems, comparable in scale to Egyptian hieroglyphs.

Several factors have hindered decipherment. No bilingual or multilingual inscriptions have been found, depriving scholars of a comparative "key" similar to the Rosetta Stone. The inscriptions are uniformly brief, offering little context for identifying grammar, vocabulary, or repetition patterns. Moreover, there is still no consensus on whether the script is logographic, syllabic, alphabetic, or a mixed system.

Recent statistical and computational analyses have shown that the symbols occur in patterned, non-random sequences, consistent with structured writing rather than decorative marking. While this supports the conclusion that the Indus people possessed a true writing system, it has not yet led to a definitive breakthrough. The script therefore remains one of the most enduring and tantalizing puzzles of ancient world archaeology.

1.4.6 Metallurgy and Trade

Archaeological research demonstrates that the Indus Valley Civilization possessed a highly developed tradition of metallurgy and was deeply embedded in regional and interregional exchange networks. Copper was the most commonly used metal and appears in a wide range of tools, weapons, and domestic vessels. Over time, the use of bronze—an alloy of copper and tin—became increasingly common, especially in later phases of the civilization. Because tin is not naturally available in the Indus region, the presence of bronze objects provides clear evidence that Indus communities were obtaining essential raw materials through long-distance trade, likely from areas in Afghanistan and Central Asia.

Alongside copper and bronze, gold was regularly employed for jewelry and personal ornaments, while silver vessels and decorative items are particularly associated with wealthier or elite contexts. Stone technology also reached a high level of specialization. Chert blades, produced through the crested guided ridge technique, were manufactured in large quantities and distributed widely. These razor-sharp cutting tools formed an important traded commodity within the Indus realm and beyond, reflecting organized production and regional exchange systems.

Trade Networks

Both archaeological finds and ancient texts attest to the extensive external trade connections of the Indus civilization. Akkadian inscriptions from Mesopotamia, dating to the reign of Sargon of Akkad (circa 2334–2279 BCE), refer to a distant land called Meluhha, widely identified by scholars as the Indus region. These inscriptions record that ships from Dilmun, Magan, and Meluhha docked at the quays of Agade, indicating that Indus merchants were directly involved in maritime commerce with Mesopotamian cities.

Material evidence supports these textual references. Indus seals and seal impressions have been recovered from Mesopotamian sites such as Ur, Babylon, and Susa, particularly in Akkadian and Ur III period contexts. The presence of cord and sack impressions on clay sealings suggests that seals were used to mark ownership and authenticate consignments of goods, pointing to a formalized system of commercial exchange.

The range of goods traded reflects clear patterns of specialization and comparative advantage. The Indus civilization exported timber, ivory, carnelian, lapis lazuli, grain, and shell and bone inlay materials—resources either scarce or highly valued in Mesopotamia. In return, Mesopotamian merchants supplied tin, silver, and woolen textiles, commodities that were difficult or impossible to obtain locally in the Indus region. This reciprocal exchange benefited both partners and sustained long-distance economic integration.

Internal Trade

In addition to overseas commerce, the Indus civilization maintained extensive internal trade networks. The Indus River and its tributaries functioned as major transportation arteries, supporting riverine traffic and facilitating movement of goods between inland and coastal regions. Archaeological evidence of warehouses and standardized weights and measures across distant sites indicates the presence of coordinated commercial practices. Such standardization would have reduced uncertainty in transactions and strengthened trust among merchants, enabling a high degree of economic integration across the Indus world.

1.5 Economic Development: The Evolution of Money

1.5.1 Introduction: How Economies Functioned

As Indian society moved from small agrarian villages to complex urban and political systems, methods of valuation and exchange evolved in parallel. Early communities initially relied on direct barter, but over time they developed more structured and symbolic mechanisms to facilitate trade, taxation, and redistribution. Historians and economists identify a sequence of monetary stages in ancient India, each responding to changing economic scales, administrative needs, and patterns of social organization.

Evidence for these stages is preserved not only in archaeological remains but also in later Vedic and post-Vedic literature, which record terminology, symbolic values, and ritual meanings attached to objects of exchange. Textual traditions such as the Rigveda and subsequent Vedic corpora refer to cattle, metals, and later standardized units as measures of wealth and payment, reflecting an evolving conception of money beyond simple barter.

These developments are further mirrored in the symbolic vocabulary of early coinage. The imagery, weights, and marking systems employed on punch-marked coins reveal continuity with older traditions of valuation and ritual symbolism, demonstrating that economic change was cumulative rather than abrupt. Together, literary and material sources provide a coherent picture of how early Indian economies gradually developed increasingly abstract and standardized forms of money, laying the foundations for later fiscal systems and state-level taxation practices.

1.5.2 The Pastoral Stage: Cattle as Currency

The earliest clearly documented economic system in ancient India is preserved in the Rigveda, one of the oldest surviving bodies of Indo-Aryan literature. These hymns depict a predominantly pastoral society in which cattle—especially cows—formed the primary measure of wealth, medium of exchange, and store of value. Economic life was so closely tied to cattle that concepts of prosperity, ownership, and status were linguistically and culturally framed around them.

Several Sanskrit terms embedded in Vedic usage reflect this centrality. The word gomat, meaning "one who possesses cattle," was synonymous with being prosperous. Pasu (cattle) was commonly employed as a general term for wealth, while gosampatti, literally "a collection of cows," denoted valuable property or accumulated assets. These linguistic patterns reveal that cattle were not merely economic resources but the very foundation of how wealth was conceptualized and expressed.

Cattle functioned in nearly all major economic and social transactions. They were transferred as bride-price in marriage arrangements, used as compensation in disputes, and offered as sacrificial gifts in religious rituals. Priests received cattle as remuneration for performing ceremonies, and the prestige of chiefs and warriors was often measured by the size of their herds. Raids and conflicts frequently targeted cattle, underscoring their value as both economic capital and symbols of power.

The prominence of cattle in the Vedic economy reflected practical realities. Herds supplied milk and dairy products, hides for leather, traction power through oxen, and meat when required. Beyond these material uses, cattle possessed qualities that made them particularly suitable as money-like assets. They were mobile, easily recognizable, capable of reproduction, and thus able to increase wealth organically. These features made cattle an efficient and trusted medium of exchange and store of value, helping to explain why pastoral societies across the world, including early Vedic India, developed similar cattle-based economic systems.

1.5.3 The Agricultural Stage: Commodity Money

As economic life in the Indian subcontinent gradually shifted from predominantly pastoral systems toward more settled agricultural economies—especially during and after the Later Vedic period—new forms of money began to supplement cattle-based wealth. While cattle retained symbolic and economic importance, communities increasingly relied on commodity money, that is, objects with socially recognized and relatively standardized value, to facilitate everyday exchange and larger commercial transactions.

Among the most widespread and enduring of these commodity currencies were cowrie shells, particularly those of Cypraea moneta. Cowries possessed a combination of qualities that made them well suited to monetary use. They were durable and did not deteriorate over time, light and portable, naturally uniform in size, and difficult to counterfeit. Because they were widely familiar across the subcontinent, cowries were easily accepted in exchange. Their monetary role proved so resilient that they continued to function as legal tender in parts of India into the nineteenth century. In Bengal, for example, an official exchange rate recorded in 1821 equated 2,568 cowrie shells to one rupee, illustrating the extraordinary longevity of this shell-based currency system.

The use of cowries in India had deep historical roots. Cowrie shells became increasingly important in regional and interregional trade. The Maldive Islands emerged as a primary source of high-quality shells, and maritime expeditions were organized specifically to collect and transport them for distribution throughout the subcontinent. This long-distance shell trade demonstrates how fully cowrie currency became embedded in Indian economic life.

In addition to shells, textiles—particularly cotton and silk cloth—served as forms of commodity money in various regions and periods. Because textiles embodied skilled labor and could be produced in standardized lengths or garments, they were widely accepted as valuable exchange items. Their relative durability and ease of storage made them practical as stores of value as well as media of exchange. Similarly, leather goods and goat-skins functioned in certain contexts as recognized units of value, further illustrating the diversity of commodity monies that developed within India's evolving agricultural economies.

Together, these commodity currencies reflect a stage in which economic exchange became increasingly abstract and standardized, paving the way for the eventual emergence of metal coinage and formal monetary systems.

1.5.4 Legacy and Continuity

The long transition from cattle-based wealth to commodity money and eventually to coined metallic currency represents one of the most significant economic developments in early Indian history. These changes were not abrupt replacements of older systems but cumulative innovations in which new forms of exchange were layered upon existing practices. As economic life became more complex and monetized, earlier conceptions of value were not erased; instead, they were absorbed into cultural memory and symbolic tradition.

The enduring cultural importance of cattle offers a clear illustration of this continuity. Although cattle gradually ceased to function as the primary medium of exchange, their symbolic and ritual value remained deeply embedded in Indian society. In Hindu tradition, the cow continues to be treated with special reverence, reflecting the ancient Vedic association between cattle, prosperity, and moral order. This reverence is not merely religious sentiment but a cultural echo of an early economic system in which cattle once embodied wealth, security, and social status.

Cowrie shells provide another powerful example. Even after they were displaced by metallic coinage and later colonial monetary systems, cowries did not lose their cultural resonance. They continued to appear in decorative, ritual, and ceremonial contexts, where they symbolized prosperity, fertility, and spiritual power. Their persistence in such roles demonstrates how deeply commodity currencies had become woven into social and religious life, long after their formal economic functions had ended.

Together, these survivals show that economic history is not simply a story of technological replacement. It is also a story of memory, symbolism, and continuity, in which older forms of value continue to shape cultural meanings and social practices long after their original economic roles have faded.

1.6 Conclusion: The Foundations of Civilization

The long historical arc stretching from the Paleolithic age to the mature phase of the Indus Valley Civilization reveals a continuous process of human adaptation, experimentation, and cumulative innovation. Across this immense span of time, communities on the Indian subcontinent transformed themselves from small groups of mobile foragers into participants in one of the world's earliest urban civilizations. Stone tool traditions, early subsistence strategies, agricultural experimentation, craft specialization, and the eventual emergence of urban centers together illustrate a sustained human effort to respond creatively to environmental constraints and social needs.

This history, however, is not a narrative of uninterrupted progress. Paleolithic life was marked by extreme vulnerability, high mortality, and constant uncertainty. The adoption of agriculture brought greater food security but also introduced new risks, including dependence on seasonal cycles and susceptibility to crop failure. Urbanization, while enabling unprecedented technological and organizational achievements, created dense living conditions that heightened exposure to disease and environmental stress. Each major transformation carried both benefits and new challenges, reshaping the balance between security and risk.

What stands out most clearly is the cumulative nature of human achievement. Innovations such as the Levallois stone-working technique, the development of polished Neolithic tools, the domestication of plants and animals, and the sophisticated drainage and sanitation systems of Indus cities were not isolated breakthroughs but the result of countless small advances refined over generations. Long-distance trade networks, standardized weights and measures, and early monetary systems further demonstrate the growing complexity of economic and social organization.

Understanding this deep and layered past enriches our appreciation of the modern world. The comforts, technologies, and social systems that shape contemporary life are rooted in solutions devised millennia ago by communities confronting uncertainty with ingenuity and persistence. The foundations of civilization were not laid in a single moment but built gradually, through sustained human effort across vast stretches of time.

Chapter 2

Vedic Age

2.1 Introduction: The Transformation of Indian Civilization Through Vedic Times

The Vedic Age marks one of the most formative phases in Indian history, encompassing two broad stages—the Early Vedic and the Later Vedic periods. Our understanding of this era is derived primarily from a rich body of Sanskrit literature, including the Vedas, Samhitas, Brahmanas, and Upanishads, which together preserve religious hymns, ritual instructions, philosophical reflections, and social norms. Far from portraying a static or unchanging society, these texts reveal a civilization in the midst of deep and sustained transformation.

During the Early Vedic period, social and economic life was predominantly pastoral and tribal in character. Communities were organized into kin-based groups, political authority was relatively decentralized, and cattle formed the central measure of wealth and social status. Settlements were largely confined to the northwestern regions of the subcontinent, especially the Punjab, and subsistence depended heavily on herding, supplemented by limited agriculture. Social relations were comparatively fluid, and political leadership was based more on personal authority and consensus than on rigid institutional structures.

Over time, however, this pastoral world underwent far-reaching change. The Later Vedic period witnessed a gradual eastward expansion into the fertile Gangetic plains, where agriculture became more intensive and sedentary settlement patterns took root. The adoption of iron technology revolutionized both farming and warfare, enabling forest clearance, increased crop yields, and the formation of more powerful political units. Tribal polities evolved into early kingdoms, trade networks expanded, and the foundations of urban life began to appear.

Simultaneously, social organization became more hierarchical. The varna system—dividing society into Brahmanas, Kshatriyas, Vaishyas, and Shudras—was increasingly formalized within religious and legal traditions, providing ideological justification for social differentiation. By the close of the Vedic Age, the subcontinent had moved decisively toward more complex political, economic, and social structures, laying the groundwork for the emergence of the mahajanapadas and the classical civilizations that would follow.

2.2 The Early Rig Vedic Period: Pastoral Life and Tribal Society

2.2.1 Introduction: Interpreting the Rigveda

The Rigveda constitutes the principal source for reconstructing the social, economic, and religious life of the Early Vedic period. It is one of the oldest surviving bodies of religious literature in the world and provides a unique insight into a predominantly pastoral and tribal society that flourished in northwestern India.

The Rigveda comprises 1,028 hymns (suktas), arranged into ten books or mandalas, and contains over 10,000 verses. These hymns were composed in Vedic Sanskrit and were preserved through a highly developed oral tradition. For centuries, they were transmitted by recitation using precise mnemonic techniques that ensured extraordinary textual accuracy long before the hymns were committed to writing. This oral discipline itself reflects the intellectual rigor and cultural priorities of early Vedic society.

It is essential to note that the Rigveda was not intended as a historical chronicle. Its primary function was liturgical: the hymns were composed to invoke deities, accompany sacrificial rituals, and express theological concepts. Nevertheless, embedded within these religious compositions are numerous references to everyday life—cattle herding, warfare, social relations, settlements, tools, and natural phenomena—which allow historians to reconstruct key features of Early Vedic society. By analyzing what the hymns praise, condemn, or take for granted, scholars can infer the economic foundations, social values, and environmental setting of the period.

The text is also composite in character. The central mandalas (Books II to VII) are generally regarded as the oldest stratum and are most closely associated with the Early Vedic phase. The remaining books—particularly I, VIII, IX, and X—contain material of mixed chronology and represent later additions or parallel traditions that were incorporated into the canonical collection. The internal organization of the Rigveda, whether by the families of seers (ṛṣis), the deities addressed, or the poetic meters employed, further indicates that deliberate editorial principles guided its compilation.

2.2.2 Geographic and Social Organization: The Punjab and Beyond

Early Vedic communities were primarily settled in the northwestern regions of the Indian subcontinent, especially in the area between the Saraswati and Drishadvati rivers. This wider region is frequently referred to in the Rigveda as Sapta Sindhu, the "land of seven rivers," a term that reflects the dense network of river systems flowing through the Punjab plains. These riverine environments offered ideal conditions for pastoral groups: seasonal pastures for grazing cattle, accessible water sources, and open tracts of land suitable for mobile herding lifestyles.

The basic social framework of Early Vedic society was the jana, a kin-based collective often rendered as a "tribe," though it functioned less as a formal political state and more as an extended lineage group united by common ancestry, language, and shared ritual traditions. Membership in a jana was defined primarily through kinship ties, which shaped social obligations, rights, and collective identity. Within each jana, smaller groupings known as viś (plural viśah) represented sub-clans or village communities, while the household formed the most immediate unit of social and economic life. The family was patriarchal in structure, with authority vested in the male head of the household, who was responsible for property, ritual duties, and decision-making.

Political organization during this period reflected the tribal and relatively egalitarian character of society. Two assemblies, the sabha and the samiti, played central roles in collective governance. The sabha functioned as a council of elders and influential members, while the samiti appears to have been a broader assembly convened to deliberate on matters of common concern. These bodies discussed issues such as inter-family disputes, decisions regarding warfare, the allocation of grazing lands, and the distribution of valuable resources. Although participation was largely restricted to senior male members and social influence was uneven, the emphasis on consultation and collective agreement indicates an early form of participatory governance. This proto-democratic arrangement contrasts with the centralized monarchical systems that would develop in later Vedic and post-Vedic periods and is repeatedly referenced in the Rigveda, underscoring its importance in early Vedic political life.

2.2.3 The Pastoral Economy: Cattle and Wealth

Economic life in the Early Rig Vedic period was firmly grounded in cattle pastoralism, which shaped not only subsistence practices but also social status, political power, and religious life. To the Vedic peoples, cattle were far more than sources of milk or meat. They constituted the principal measure of wealth and prosperity and served as the foundation of economic value. This centrality is reflected clearly in Vedic language and terminology, where ideas of wealth and success are consistently expressed through references to cattle.

Several key Sanskrit expressions demonstrate how deeply cattle-based thinking permeated Vedic society. The term gomat ("one who possesses cows") functioned as a synonym for a prosperous and respected person. Pasu (cattle) was widely used to denote wealth itself, while gosampatti—literally a "collection of cows"—referred to accumulated property and material abundance. Linguistically and culturally, to be wealthy was to own cattle, to be generous was to distribute cows, and to lack cattle was to be poor. Economic vocabulary thus reveals that cattle formed the very language of wealth in Early Vedic consciousness.

The dominance of cattle can be explained by their exceptional economic utility. Herds provided milk, curds, butter, and ghee—nutritious and storable foods essential for survival in a pastoral environment. Hides were used to produce leather for clothing, containers, straps, and shelter coverings. As mobile assets, cattle could be moved with migrating groups, allowing wealth to be preserved during periods of conflict or ecological stress. Moreover, cattle reproduced naturally, enabling wealth to grow without fresh capital investment. Their visibility further reinforced their role as currency-like assets, since the size of a household's herd could be readily observed and assessed by others.

Beyond material utility, cattle possessed profound ritual and symbolic value. They were central to sacrificial ceremonies, served as offerings to the gods, and functioned as prestigious gifts bestowed upon priests and warriors. The success of chiefs was often measured by the number of cattle they owned or distributed. Inter-tribal conflicts frequently revolved around cattle acquisition, a reality captured in the Rigvedic term gaviṣṭi, literally "the search for cows," used to denote warfare. The concept of gaupratiharya, referring to cattle protection, further highlights how safeguarding herds was a major social concern.

The Rigveda itself reflects a society in which cattle-based wealth could be acquired through diverse forms of labor. A well-known verse (Rigveda IX.112) speaks of a family engaged in different occupations yet united in their aspiration to gain wealth through various activities, suggesting both occupational flexibility and a broadly shared desire for prosperity measured in cattle. In this way, cattle functioned simultaneously as economic capital, social status markers, ritual offerings, and symbols of prosperity—playing a role analogous to currency in later monetary economies.

2.2.4 Animal Husbandry: Diversity Beyond Cattle

Although cattle formed the core of Early Vedic economic life, pastoral communities did not rely on a single species alone. The Rigveda makes repeated reference to a variety of domesticated animals, indicating that herding practices were diversified and adapted to meet different subsistence, technological, and social needs. This diversity strengthened economic resilience by ensuring that households were not entirely dependent on one type of livestock.

Sheep and goats are mentioned in the hymns and were valued primarily for their wool, hides, and meat. Wool production is implied through references to

2.2. THE EARLY RIG VEDIC PERIOD: PASTORAL LIFE AND TRIBAL SOCIETY

weaving and woven garments, suggesting that textile manufacture was already an established domestic craft. These animals provided renewable materials essential for clothing and coverings, contributing significantly to household self-sufficiency.

Horses occupied a particularly prestigious position within Early Vedic society. Rather than serving as ordinary beasts of burden, they were closely associated with warfare, chariotry, and elite status. Chariots drawn by horses enabled rapid movement and played a decisive role in conflict, giving military advantage to those who possessed superior animals. Horse racing and ritual competitions further elevated the symbolic value of horses. The Aśvamedha (horse sacrifice), one of the most elaborate royal rituals described in Vedic literature, illustrates the political and religious importance attached to these animals. Ownership of fine horses thus became a marker of wealth, authority, and social distinction.

Oxen and bullocks formed the principal sources of traction power. They pulled wagons, assisted in transport, and could also be slaughtered for meat when required. Dogs are also mentioned in the hymns and were likely employed for herding and hunting, supporting both pastoral management and subsistence activities.

This diversified livestock economy reduced vulnerability to environmental or social disruptions. Should cattle herds suffer losses due to disease, drought, or conflict, other animals could continue to supply food, labor, and materials. In this way, Early Vedic pastoralism was not only economically productive but also strategically adaptive, enabling communities to manage risk while maintaining social stability.

2.2.5 Supplementary Agriculture: The Secondary Economy

Although pastoralism formed the backbone of Early Vedic economic life, agriculture was not absent. The Rigveda contains clear references to cultivated crops, indicating that early Vedic communities practiced farming as a supplementary subsistence activity alongside herding. Barley appears most prominently in the hymns and was likely the principal cultivated grain, while wheat and other cereals are also mentioned, suggesting a basic but functional agricultural tradition.

The overall subsistence pattern points to a form of semi-nomadic pastoralism. Vedic groups appear to have moved seasonally with their herds in search of fresh pasture and water, but they also remained in favorable locations long enough to cultivate crops. During these settled intervals, fields were prepared, seeds were sown, and crops were tended until harvest. This mixed strategy—combining mobility with periodic cultivation—allowed communities to balance the flexibility of herding with the food security provided by farming.

Textual references confirm that agricultural techniques were known and practiced. The Rigveda mentions ploughing, and specific hymns refer to the preparation and working of fields (for example, Rigveda 3.29.1). The term kārṣaka was used for those engaged in tilling the soil, indicating a recognized occupational role connected with farming activities.

Nevertheless, the relatively limited number of agricultural references in the Rigveda, when compared to the extensive pastoral imagery and terminology, suggests that farming played a secondary role in Early Vedic society. Herding remained the dominant economic foundation, while agriculture functioned primarily as a supporting activity. Over time, however, this balance shifted. Later Vedic literature increasingly emphasizes cultivation and settled agricultural life, reflecting a gradual transition toward more intensive farming and permanent settlement patterns in subsequent periods.

2.2.6 Craft Production and Occupational Specialization

As Early Vedic society became more socially and economically differentiated, a gradual process of occupational specialization began to emerge. Although professions were not yet rigidly fixed by birth or hereditary status, the Rigveda and associated Vedic texts clearly attest to the presence of recognized crafts and specialized forms of labor. Individuals could shift occupations according to skill, opportunity, and circumstance, reflecting a relatively flexible economic order in which aptitude rather than lineage primarily determined one's livelihood [32][35].

Metallurgical specialists already occupied an important place in Early Vedic society. The term ayas in the Rigveda denotes copper and bronze, indicating familiarity with non-ferrous metallurgy well before the introduction of iron. Smiths fashioned tools, weapons, and ornaments, and their craft was held in high regard. Vedic hymns refer to the smith as a valued figure, highlighting his role in producing essential implements and objects of prestige.

Woodworkers formed another vital occupational group. Carpenters were responsible for constructing wagons used in pastoral transport, as well as chariots, which represented the most advanced military technology of the period. Chariots, drawn by horses, were central to warfare and elite display, and those who possessed the technical knowledge to build and maintain them enjoyed considerable respect. The frequent mention of chariots and chariotry in the Rigveda underscores their social and military importance.

Textile specialists, particularly women, played a major role in domestic and economic life. Wool obtained from sheep was spun into thread and woven into cloth, and references to woven garments appear repeatedly in Vedic hymns. Weaving required skill and time, and the presence of specialized weavers indicates an emerging division of labor within households and communities.

Beyond these major crafts, the texts mention a wide range of other specialized occupations. Physicians (bhiṣaj) are referred to, suggesting the existence of medical knowledge and healing practices. Barbers, leather workers, and potters performed essential services, while hunters and fishermen exploited wild and aquatic resources to supplement pastoral and agricultural food supplies.

References to traders indicate that exchange between communities was already occurring and required intermediaries to facilitate the movement of goods.

What is particularly significant is the apparent social openness of Early Vedic occupational life. Unlike later periods, in which occupations became rigidly hereditary and hierarchically ranked, Early Vedic society shows little evidence of occupational stigma. Individuals were not bound to their parents' professions, and families could include members engaged in different livelihoods. A well-known Rigvedic verse explicitly mentions a household in which the father is a physician, the mother a grain-grinder, and the son a priestly reciter, illustrating that occupational mobility was socially acceptable and that skill and opportunity played decisive roles in shaping economic life.

2.2.7 Trade and Exchange: Local Commerce and Long-Distance Networks

Exchange in the Early Vedic period was largely organized on a local and regional scale and operated primarily through barter. In the absence of standardized coinage or formally defined currency, goods were traded directly for other goods perceived to be of comparable value. Within this system, cattle functioned as the principal standard of valuation. Because herds represented universally recognized wealth, prices and obligations could be expressed in terms of cows—for example, in statements equivalent to "worth so many cattle." In this way, cattle served not only as productive assets but also as the chief medium of exchange and store of value within everyday economic transactions.

The Rigveda also refers to gold ornaments and precious objects, indicating that gold had begun to acquire recognized value as a luxury material and as a prestigious form of wealth. However, gold does not appear to have functioned as a standardized or widely circulating medium of exchange in the Early Vedic period. Its use seems to have been more closely associated with gifts, ritual offerings, and displays of status rather than routine market transactions.

References in the later hymns of the Rigveda also suggest the early appearance of cowrie shells as portable objects of value. Their small size, durability, and natural uniformity made them suitable for exchange, although clear and systematic evidence for their use as formal money becomes much stronger in the Later Vedic and post-Vedic periods. These early mentions may represent the initial stages of a monetary tradition that would later become deeply embedded in Indian economic life.

Beyond local exchange, there are indications that Early Vedic communities were not entirely isolated from wider commercial worlds. While the Later Vedic period provides more explicit evidence for long-distance trade, some scholarly interpretations suggest that the foundations of interregional contacts—possibly extending toward West Asia—may already have been taking shape during the Early Vedic era. These early connections, even if limited, hint at the gradual integration of Vedic society into broader networks of exchange that would expand significantly in subsequent centuries.

2.2.8 Social Structure: The Emergence of Status Differentiation

Although Early Vedic society is often characterized as relatively egalitarian when compared with later Hindu social formations, the Rigveda itself reveals clear patterns of emerging status differentiation. Social life was not uniform, and distinctions of wealth, power, and prestige were already taking shape within tribal communities.

At the top of this hierarchy stood an elite group composed primarily of wealthy cattle-owners and warrior leaders. The hymns frequently refer to rājas, variously translated as chiefs or kings, who exercised military leadership and political authority within their respective janas. These leaders controlled larger herds, presided over important rituals, led war expeditions, and received tribute and gifts from their followers. Their elevated position was therefore supported both by economic resources—particularly cattle wealth—and by control over armed force.

Closely associated with the warrior elite were the priests, who constituted a learned class responsible for preserving sacred knowledge and conducting ritual life. The early formation of the Brahminical tradition is visible in the importance attached to ritual specialists who memorized hymns, supervised sacrifices, and interpreted religious procedures. Their services were highly valued, and they were regularly compensated with gifts, especially cattle, reinforcing their elevated social standing.

Below these elite groups lay a broad body of free herders and cultivators who formed the main productive population. At the lower end of the social spectrum were individuals and groups who lacked significant property and were dependent on others for subsistence. These landless or servile persons could be required to perform labor and service, though the Rigveda does not yet present these distinctions as rigid, hereditary castes.

Importantly, social position in Early Vedic society was not entirely fixed by birth. While family background mattered, individuals could improve their status through the accumulation of cattle wealth, success in warfare, or mastery of ritual knowledge. This relative flexibility distinguishes Early Vedic society from the more rigidly stratified systems that would develop in later Vedic and classical periods, highlighting a transitional phase in the evolution of social hierarchy.

2.2.9 The Role of Women in Early Vedic Society

The position of women in Early Vedic society reflects a comparatively open and participatory social environment, especially when contrasted with the more restrictive norms that developed in later periods of Indian history. Evidence

2.2. THE EARLY RIG VEDIC PERIOD: PASTORAL LIFE AND TRIBAL SOCIETY

preserved in the Rigveda indicates that women were not confined solely to domestic roles but were active participants in religious, intellectual, and social life.

One of the most striking indicators of women's status is the presence of female seers, known as ṛṣikās, whose hymns form part of the Rigvedic corpus. These women were recognized as inspired composers and transmitters of sacred knowledge. Figures such as Gārgī and Maitreyī are remembered for their intellectual and spiritual authority, demonstrating that women could attain high religious prestige and contribute directly to the formation of Vedic religious tradition. Their inclusion in sacred literature underscores that spiritual insight was not restricted to men alone.

Within the household economy, women played essential productive roles. Spinning and weaving were widely acknowledged as women's work, and the manufacture of woolen textiles required considerable skill and labor. These activities were fundamental to household self-sufficiency and carried recognized economic value. Women also participated in domestic ritual practices and were not excluded from religious observance. The Rigveda contains references to women attending assemblies and taking part in public festivals, suggesting that their presence in communal life was socially accepted.

At the same time, the sources also reveal early signs of gender hierarchy. Although some women are remembered as seers, the vast majority of hymns are attributed to male composers, and references to family organization point toward a patrilineal structure in which descent and inheritance followed the male line. Marriage practices indicate the gradual consolidation of male authority within households. These tendencies became more pronounced in the Later Vedic period, when women's social and ritual roles were increasingly circumscribed.

Thus, Early Vedic society presents a nuanced picture: women enjoyed a degree of religious participation, intellectual recognition, and social visibility that would later diminish, even as the foundations of a more patriarchal order were already beginning to take shape.

2.2.10 Ritual and Religion: Sacrifice as the Center of Life

Religious life in the Early Vedic period revolved around the practice of yajña, or sacrifice, which functioned as the central mechanism linking human society to the divine order. In Vedic thought, sacrifice was not merely an act of devotion but a reciprocal transaction between humans and the gods. By offering valued substances—such as cattle, grain, clarified butter (ghṛta or ghee), and the sacred soma juice—to particular deities, worshippers sought divine favor in the form of protection, prosperity, victory, fertility, and social well-being. Sacrifice was thus understood as the means by which cosmic balance was maintained and human desires were fulfilled.

The most fundamental household ritual was the Agnihotra, performed twice daily by those who could afford it. In this rite, offerings of milk and ghee were made into the sacred fire dedicated to Agni, the fire god who acted as the divine messenger carrying offerings to other deities. The Agnihotra was simple in form but profound in meaning, serving as the everyday religious duty of the householder and reinforcing a continuous relationship between the domestic sphere and the cosmic order.

In addition to these domestic observances, more elaborate public sacrifices were sponsored by tribal chiefs and wealthy patrons. These rituals were performed to secure divine support for specific aims such as military success, acquisition of wealth, fertility, and political prestige. Such sacrifices often involved the offering of valuable animals—especially cattle—and required the participation of trained priests who possessed detailed knowledge of ritual sequences, sacred formulas, and ceremonial procedures. Correct performance was believed to generate tangible benefits, whereas errors could nullify the desired effects or even provoke divine displeasure.

The Rigvedic hymns themselves constituted the verbal and symbolic core of sacrificial practice. Their recitation accompanied physical offerings and ritual actions, activating the power of the sacrifice. Through praise, invocation, and formal requests, the hymns reminded the gods of their past benevolence and sought renewed favor. The structured poetic form and repeated imagery were understood to carry intrinsic potency, making speech itself a sacred instrument within Early Vedic religious life.

2.2.11 The Role of Horses and Warfare

Although Early Vedic society was not exclusively oriented toward warfare, conflict occupied a visible and symbolically charged place in its cultural life, as reflected in the Rigveda. Inter-tribal competition over resources—especially cattle, grazing lands, and access to water—frequently gave rise to raids and armed encounters. Within this context, warfare became an important means through which wealth and prestige could be acquired.

The horse played a decisive role in Early Vedic warfare. Unlike oxen, which were primarily valued for traction and agricultural labor, horses were prized for their speed and strength, making them ideal for mounted combat and for drawing light chariots. Mastery over horses and chariotry distinguished the warrior elite, enabling rapid movement across terrain and conferring tactical advantage in battle. The possession of fine horses therefore became closely associated with political authority, military leadership, and high social status.

The Rigveda contains numerous references to cattle raids, tribal conflicts, and heroic victories. These hymns often celebrate successful warriors who returned with captured cattle and spoils, reinforcing the close connection between martial success and material prosperity. Central to this martial worldview is the god Indra, portrayed as a powerful warrior deity who defeats enemies and distributes

2.2. THE EARLY RIG VEDIC PERIOD: PASTORAL LIFE AND TRIBAL SOCIETY

wealth to his followers. Indra's exploits provided a divine model for human warriors and legitimized the pursuit of victory and booty through armed conflict.

At the same time, the prominence of warfare in the hymns should not be taken to mean that everyday life was constantly dominated by violence. The poetic and ritual nature of the Rigveda tends to emphasize dramatic episodes and heroic ideals. While conflict was a recurrent and socially significant concern, most members of Early Vedic society were likely more regularly engaged in pastoral, agricultural, and domestic activities. Warfare, though important, formed only one aspect of a broader and more varied social world.

2.2.12 Social Mobility and Merit in Early Vedic Society

One of the most distinctive features of Early Vedic society, especially when contrasted with later classical Hindu civilization, was its relative openness to social mobility based on personal achievement and merit. Occupational roles were not yet rigidly hereditary, and individuals were not bound to follow the professions of their fathers. Wealth and prestige could be accumulated through success in pastoral management, skill in craftsmanship, achievement in warfare, or mastery of ritual knowledge. In this social environment, talent, enterprise, and reputation offered genuine avenues for improving one's position within the community.

Vedic literature itself preserves explicit acknowledgment of this flexibility. A well-known hymn of the Rigveda describes members of a single household engaged in different occupations, illustrating that family lineage did not strictly determine economic or social roles. This reflects a society in which functional specialization existed, but occupational inheritance was not yet formalized as a rigid social rule.

The Purusha Sukta (Rigveda 10.90), which later became a foundational text for the varna system, is particularly revealing in its early form. The hymn employs a cosmic metaphor in which the four social categories—Brahmana, Kshatriya, Vaishya, and Shudra—are compared to different parts of the cosmic being Purusha. In its original conceptual framework, these divisions appear to be organized around social function rather than immutable birth status. The hymn does not explicitly present varna as a closed hereditary system, leaving room for functional interpretation and potential movement between categories based on occupation and role.

This relative flexibility would gradually diminish in later centuries, as social categories hardened into birth-based castes with increasingly rigid boundaries. Nevertheless, during the Early Vedic period, social identity remained comparatively fluid, allowing individuals to negotiate their status through economic success, ritual authority, and military achievement.

2.3 The Later Vedic Period: Expansion, Urbanization, and Rigidification

2.3.1 Introduction: The Changed World

The Later Vedic period marks a decisive turning point in the evolution of Indian civilization. During these centuries, the relatively mobile, pastoral, and tribal society of the Early Vedic age was transformed into a more complex and territorially organized world of kingdoms, expanding settlements, emerging urban centers, and increasingly formal political institutions. This transformation was accompanied by important technological developments, most notably the growing use of iron, which reshaped agriculture, warfare, and patterns of settlement.

Literary evidence for this period is preserved in later portions of the Vedic corpus. While some hymns in the Rigveda (particularly in Books I, VIII, IX, and X) reflect developments of this era, the clearest picture emerges from the Yajurveda and Samaveda Samhitas, as well as from the Brahmana texts and references in the Atharvaveda. Together, these sources document a society in transition—more stratified, more ritually elaborate, and more politically organized than before.

The Brahmanas are especially significant for understanding this changed world. These prose commentaries on Vedic hymns provide detailed prescriptions for ritual performance and reveal a growing preoccupation with ceremonial precision and priestly authority. Texts such as the Śatapatha Brahmana, traditionally associated with Yājñavalkya, describe highly elaborate sacrificial rites and incorporate mythological and speculative material. Although compiled later, they preserve traditions that reflect the ritual intensification characteristic of the Later Vedic age. Through these works, it becomes clear that religious life had become increasingly specialized, with ritual expertise concentrated in the hands of trained priests whose correct performance of ceremonies was believed to possess immense transformative power.

At the same time, Vedic thought began to move in new philosophical directions. The Upanishads, which form the culminating layer of the Vedic tradition, represent a shift from exclusive emphasis on external sacrifice toward introspective inquiry and spiritual knowledge. Texts such as the Chandogya, Taittirīya, and Mundaka Upanishads explore questions concerning the nature of ultimate reality (Brahman), the individual self (Ātman), and liberation (mokṣa). While rooted in earlier traditions, these works reflect the intellectual ferment of the Later Vedic and early post-Vedic periods, revealing a society increasingly concerned with metaphysical speculation alongside ritual practice.

Together, these literary developments mirror broader social changes: growing political centralization, the consolidation of hierarchical social structures, and the gradual movement toward urbanized and state-based forms of civilization.

2.3.2 Geographic Expansion: From Punjab to the Gangetic Plains

One of the most significant developments of the Later Vedic period was the steady eastward movement of Vedic-speaking communities from their earlier heartland in the Punjab and northwestern regions into the fertile valleys of the eastern Gangetic plain. Literary evidence, particularly from the Śatapatha Brāhmaṇa, explicitly refers to this expansion and records the gradual occupation of territories along the Yamuna, the Ganges, and their tributaries. These accounts make it clear that while Early Vedic society had been largely confined to the Sapta Sindhu region, the Later Vedic age witnessed systematic settlement and political consolidation further east.

This movement was driven primarily by ecological and economic incentives. The Gangetic plain offered exceptionally fertile alluvial soil deposited annually by river floods, creating ideal conditions for intensive agriculture. In contrast to the relatively semi-arid Punjab plains, which had favored pastoral and mixed subsistence strategies, the eastern river valleys could sustain dense farming populations and produce substantial agricultural surplus. These environmental advantages made the region highly attractive for expanding communities seeking more reliable and productive lands.

As successive waves of settlement moved into the Yamuna–Ganges basin, the demographic and cultural center of Vedic civilization gradually shifted eastward. New settlements, villages, and early towns began to emerge, laying the groundwork for the later rise of the mahajanapadas and the urban cultures of the early historic period. This geographic reorientation was therefore not merely a change in location but a fundamental transformation in the economic and social foundations of Vedic society, ushering in an era of intensified agriculture, political centralization, and growing urbanization.

2.3.3 The Rise of Kingdoms: From Tribal Confederacies to Monarchical States

As Vedic communities expanded eastward and settled more permanently in the Gangetic plains, older tribal confederacies gradually gave way to territorially defined political units known as janapadas—literally, "the footholds of peoples." These janapadas represented early forms of kingdoms in which political authority became increasingly centralized and hereditary ruling dynasties began to emerge. This shift marks a decisive movement away from kin-based tribal leadership toward monarchical state structures.

Among the earliest and most influential of these kingdoms were the Kuru and Pañchāla polities of the western Gangetic region. The Kurus, in particular, played a formative role in shaping Later Vedic political and religious traditions. Rulers such as Parikṣit and Janamejaya are repeatedly mentioned in Vedic literature, suggesting their prominence in both political life and ritual patronage.

The Kurus also became major patrons of Brahmanical ritualism, contributing to the consolidation of orthodox Vedic practices.

The Pañchāla kingdom emerged as another major power, especially under rulers such as Pravāhaṇa Jaivali, who became renowned for supporting learning and philosophical inquiry. Pañchāla territory was closely associated with the development of Vedic ritualism and speculative thought. In later phases, other important kingdoms rose to prominence, including Kosala, Kāśi (with its capital at Vārāṇasī), and Videha. Videha's legendary king Janaka transformed his capital, Mithilā, into a celebrated center of learning and debate, closely associated with the sage Yājñavalkya, whose teachings are preserved in major Brahmana and Upanishadic texts.

Further east, in the region of present-day Bihar, powerful polities such as Magadha, Anga, and Vanga began to take shape. These eastern kingdoms would later assume decisive importance in early historic India, particularly with the rise of Magadha as the nucleus of imperial formations such as the Mauryan state.

The expansion and consolidation of these kingdoms were accompanied by the development of increasingly complex administrative structures. Traditional offices such as the purohita (royal priest and adviser), senānī (military commander), and grāmaṇī (village head) continued to function, but new officials emerged to manage taxation, treasury, and other administrative responsibilities. The governance of larger territories required more systematic methods of revenue collection, record keeping, and resource control, signaling the gradual emergence of state-level administration in the Later Vedic world.

2.3.4 Territorial Expansion and Ritual Legitimation of Power

As political authority became increasingly centralized in the Later Vedic period, kings turned to elaborate public rituals to legitimize, display, and reinforce their sovereignty. Royal power was no longer grounded solely in personal prowess or kinship ties but was increasingly sanctified through formalized sacrificial ceremonies that linked political authority to divine approval.

The Rājasūya ceremony served as the ritual of royal consecration. Through this rite, a ruler's authority was formally established or reaffirmed, symbolically transforming him from a tribal leader into a divinely sanctioned monarch. The ceremony emphasized the king's role as the pivot of social and cosmic order, legitimizing his right to rule in both religious and political terms.

The most elaborate and prestigious of these rituals was the Aśvamedha, or horse sacrifice. A consecrated horse was released to wander freely across neighboring territories. If rival rulers failed to capture it, they tacitly acknowledged the supremacy of the sponsoring king. The eventual sacrificial offering of the horse required immense material resources and complex ritual performance, making the Aśvamedha a powerful public demonstration of wealth, military strength,

2.3. THE LATER VEDIC PERIOD: EXPANSION, URBANIZATION, AND RIGIDIFICATION

and divine favor. Only the most powerful kings could afford to undertake such a ceremony, and its successful completion proclaimed their paramount status.

Another important royal rite was the Vājapeya, literally meaning "the drink of strength." This ceremony included a series of elaborate ritual actions, among which a chariot race was particularly significant, with the king symbolically expected to emerge victorious. Like the Aśvamedha, the Vājapeya functioned as a public affirmation of royal vigor, legitimacy, and divine sanction [38].

Collectively, these royal sacrifices served multiple social and political functions. They publicly displayed royal power and wealth, reinforced the king's sacred status, integrated subordinate chiefs and communities into a hierarchical political order, and facilitated the redistribution of resources through gifts, feasting, and ritual generosity. In this way, ritual practice became a central instrument for consolidating territorial expansion and transforming tribal leadership into institutionalized monarchy in the Later Vedic world.

2.3.5 The Iron Age: Technology and Transformation

One of the most decisive developments of the Later Vedic period was the growing adoption of iron technology. Unlike copper and bronze, which depended on relatively scarce ores and complex alloying processes, iron was far more abundant in the Indian subcontinent. Once the techniques of smelting, forging, and hardening were mastered, iron tools and weapons could be produced in larger quantities and at lower cost. This made metal implements more accessible beyond elite circles and introduced a new technological foundation for both warfare and economic activity.

Militarily, iron brought significant advantages. Iron-tipped spears, swords, and armor were stronger and more durable than their bronze counterparts. Archaeological finds from sites such as Hastinapura and Ujjain include substantial quantities of iron weapons and tools dated to the Later Vedic period, confirming the textual evidence for widespread use. Access to iron ore and skilled smiths provided strategic advantages to emerging kingdoms. The political ascendancy of polities such as the Kurus and Pañchālas is closely associated with their early adoption of iron weaponry, which strengthened their military capacity relative to groups still dependent on bronze and stone implements.

Agriculturally, the impact of iron was significant but more gradual and complex than once assumed. Although iron ploughshares and cutting tools were technologically superior to wooden or stone implements, much agricultural equipment continued to be made from traditional materials for a considerable time. The major agricultural expansion of the Later Vedic period was driven less by immediate replacement of ploughs and more by enhanced forest clearance—made possible by iron axes—along with improvements in irrigation and diversification of crops. These changes opened new tracts of land for cultivation and supported the growth of settled farming communities.

In aggregate, iron technology facilitated wide-ranging social and economic transformation. More efficient tools aided land clearance and construction, supporting population growth and permanent settlement. Cheaper and more durable weapons reinforced political consolidation and territorial expansion. Over time, iron-working itself became a specialized craft, and smiths emerged as recognized members of the social and economic order. Through these cumulative effects, iron contributed fundamentally to the transformation of Later Vedic society into a more complex, agrarian, and state-organized civilization.

2.3.6 Agriculture: Becoming the Dominant Subsistence Strategy

The Later Vedic period marked a decisive transformation in the economic foundations of society, as agriculture replaced pastoralism as the principal subsistence strategy. This shift was closely linked to the eastward expansion into the fertile Gangetic plains, where rich alluvial soils and dependable water supplies encouraged settled cultivation. Texts such as the Śatapatha Brāhmaṇa contain frequent references to farming, village life, and land use, reflecting the growing centrality of agriculture in everyday economic activity.

A wide range of crops was cultivated during this period. Barley and wheat continued to be important staples, especially in the western regions, while rice became increasingly prominent in the eastern Gangetic plains. Pulses such as lentils and peas supplemented cereal production, and millets provided additional grain resources. The cultivation of cotton indicates the integration of agriculture with textile production, and sugarcane appears with increasing frequency in later phases, reflecting diversification of agricultural output. These varied crops suggest a maturing agricultural economy capable of supporting large and stable populations.

The agricultural calendar came to structure social life, replacing the earlier pastoral seasonal rhythm. Communities organized labor around cycles of ploughing, sowing, irrigation, and harvest, and most households became tied to specific plots of land for at least part of the year. Permanent villages grew in number and size, forming the basic units of Later Vedic settlement and administration.

This transformation was gradual rather than abrupt. Cattle remained economically and symbolically important, providing traction for ploughing and transport and continuing to hold ritual significance. However, the primary measure of wealth and power increasingly shifted from control over herds to control over land and agricultural surplus. These surpluses supported the growth of non-food-producing specialists—priests, administrators, artisans, and traders—thereby enabling greater occupational specialization and contributing to the emergence of more complex social and political structures.

2.3. THE LATER VEDIC PERIOD: EXPANSION, URBANIZATION, AND RIGIDIFICATION47

2.3.7 Urbanization: The Emergence of Cities

Archaeological data, together with literary references, point to the gradual formation of a network of urban centers across the Gangetic plains and adjoining regions. Among the earliest and most prominent were Ayodhya (the capital of Kosala), Vārāṇasī/Kāśī (capital of Kāśī), Mithilā (capital of Videha), Ujjain in central India, Champa in the eastern regions, and Śrāvastī, which became an important center of learning during the Later Vedic and early post-Vedic periods.

They represented significant concentrations of population, production, and exchange. Within these urban environments, occupational specialization expanded rapidly. Crafts such as pottery making, metallurgy, weaving, cart construction, brewing, and other artisanal activities flourished, forming the economic backbone of urban communities. Markets and workshops became permanent features of city life, while merchants facilitated the circulation of goods between urban centers and their rural hinterlands.

Cities also developed as intellectual and cultural hubs. Priests, teachers, and scholars established themselves in urban settings, attracting students and patrons and contributing to the growth of educational and religious institutions. This concentration of learning further distinguished urban centers from surrounding rural settlements.

Archaeological excavations, particularly at sites such as Hastinapura, provide material confirmation of these developments. Planned street layouts, specialized craft areas, and storage facilities for grain indicate organized urban management. Pottery assemblages from different Later Vedic sites display shared styles and technological similarities, suggesting regular exchange and communication between regions. Together, these features reveal the emergence of interconnected urban networks that formed the foundation of early historic city life in northern India.

2.3.8 Trade and Commerce: Expanding Networks

The Later Vedic period saw a marked expansion in systems of trade and exchange, both within the subcontinent and beyond it. Literary and archaeological evidence indicates that Vedic polities were increasingly integrated into wider commercial networks that connected northern India with distant regions of West Asia. Later Vedic texts make reference to the exchange of high-value goods such as timber, ivory, precious stones, and spices, which were traded for commodities unavailable locally, including tin—essential for bronze production—and silver obtained from foreign lands.

Trade with Mesopotamia appears to have been mediated through established maritime and overland routes. The Persian Gulf region, particularly Dilmun (identified with ancient Bahrain), functioned as a major entrepôt through which goods from India, Mesopotamia, and neighboring regions were exchanged. References in Sanskrit literature to foreign merchants and distant lands become more frequent in Later Vedic sources, indicating a growing awareness of, and participation in, interregional commerce.

Within the subcontinent, expanding trade networks linked the various Vedic kingdoms into an increasingly interconnected economic system. Major rivers such as the Ganges and Yamuna served as natural transport corridors, facilitating riverine trade that was more efficient than overland movement. At important nodal points, ports, warehouses, and market centers developed to support storage, redistribution, and exchange of goods. Evidence also suggests a gradual move toward more standardized forms of exchange, with cowrie shells gaining wider acceptance as a medium of value in transactions that extended beyond simple barter, marking an important step toward more formal monetary practices.

Together, these developments reflect a growing commercialization of the Later Vedic economy and the gradual integration of Vedic society into long-distance networks of trade and exchange that would become even more prominent in the early historic period.

2.3.9 Occupational Specialization and the Crafts

The economic expansion and growing urbanization of the Later Vedic period encouraged a far higher degree of occupational specialization than had existed earlier. As agriculture generated reliable surpluses, many individuals were freed from direct food production and were able to devote themselves full-time to skilled crafts. Towns and emerging cities became the principal centers of such specialized activity, where craftspeople could exchange their products for food and other necessities through expanding market networks. References scattered across the Rigveda, Yajurveda, and Atharvaveda attest to the diversity and complexity of these occupations.

Metalworkers assumed a particularly prominent role. With the growing use of iron alongside copper and bronze, smiths were required to master increasingly complex metallurgical techniques—smelting ore, forging tools and weapons, and hardening or tempering metal for durability. These skills were highly valued and were typically transmitted within families or closely knit occupational groups, ensuring continuity of technical knowledge.

Leather workers and tanners processed hides into a wide range of goods, including footwear, clothing, armor, and containers. Potters produced ceramic vessels in expanding varieties of form and finish, reflecting both functional needs and growing aesthetic refinement. Weavers supplied textiles for domestic use and for trade, and Indian cloth became an increasingly important commodity in interregional exchange networks.

Carpenters and woodworkers continued to be essential, producing chariots, carts, boats, and structural components for houses and public buildings. Brewers and producers of fermented drinks are also mentioned in Vedic texts, indicating that

2.3. THE LATER VEDIC PERIOD: EXPANSION, URBANIZATION, AND RIGIDIFICATION

alcoholic beverages had become established items of production and consumption. In addition, the literature refers to a range of other specialists, including performers, physicians, and scholars, underscoring the widening spectrum of professional activity.

A significant social change accompanied this growth in specialization. During the Later Vedic period, many occupations began to show a stronger tendency toward hereditary transmission, with sons commonly following the professions of their fathers. Although social categories were not yet fully rigid, this trend toward hereditary specialization marked an important step in the gradual formation of more fixed occupational groups, laying part of the foundation for the later caste system.

2.3.10 The Varna System: Codification of Social Hierarchy

One of the most far-reaching social transformations of the Later Vedic age was the gradual codification of hierarchy into the varna system. The earliest textual expression of this fourfold social division appears in the Puruṣa Sūkta (Rigveda 10.90), which presents social differentiation through a cosmic metaphor. The hymn describes the primordial being Puruṣa as having been ritually sacrificed, and from different parts of his body emerged the four social categories: Brahmins from the mouth, Kshatriyas from the arms, Vaishyas from the thighs, and Shudras from the feet. This imagery provided a religious framework for understanding and justifying social order.

In its earliest conception, the varna scheme appears primarily as a functional division of labor rather than a rigid hereditary system. Each group was defined by its social role—Brahmins as ritual specialists and scholars, Kshatriyas as rulers and warriors, Vaishyas as cultivators, herders, and traders, and Shudras as service providers. Over the course of the Later Vedic and Brahmanic periods, however, these functional categories became increasingly associated with birth, and social mobility based on personal achievement gradually diminished.

The Brahmins rose to occupy the highest position within this hierarchy. Their authority rested on their exclusive mastery of Vedic ritual knowledge and their indispensable role in performing sacrifices believed to sustain cosmic and social order. Brahmana texts, especially the Śatapatha Brāhmaṇa, repeatedly emphasize the necessity of Brahmin participation in major rituals and affirm their elevated status. By the Later Vedic period, Brahmin identity had become largely hereditary, even though in principle access to Vedic learning through initiation and discipleship was still acknowledged.

The Kshatriyas constituted the ruling and warrior elite. They exercised political authority, commanded armies, and sponsored major royal sacrifices. Their prestige derived from military success and governance, and while early status may have depended on achievement, Later Vedic developments increasingly tied Kshatriya identity to birth within recognized royal and warrior lineages.

The Vaishyas formed the broad productive base of society, encompassing cultivators, pastoralists, merchants, and artisans. This economically vital group generated agricultural surplus and commercial wealth. Vaishyas enjoyed social respect but remained hierarchically subordinate to Brahmins and Kshatriyas. Over time, Vaishya identity also tended toward hereditary definition, particularly among prosperous farming and merchant families.

The Shudras occupied the lowest of the four varnas. Their designated role was to serve the three higher groups. Many were likely descendants of populations incorporated into expanding Vedic polities. From early stages of varna codification, Shudras were excluded from key ritual privileges: they could not undergo the sacred thread ceremony (upanayana), were barred from hearing Vedic recitation, and were restricted from participating fully in ritual life. Their position became increasingly subordinated as varna distinctions hardened.

Beyond the fourfold scheme existed a fifth and marginal category, often referred to as Pañchamas or later "untouchables." These groups were associated with occupations considered ritually polluting, such as handling the dead or working with hides, and they were placed outside the formal varna order, facing severe social and ritual exclusion.

It is important to note that although the foundations of this hierarchical system were laid during the Later Vedic period, absolute rigidity had not yet fully set in. Vedic references still preserve traces of occupational flexibility and social mobility. However, later legal and normative texts—most notably the Manusmṛti—would transform these early functional distinctions into a far more rigid, birth-based caste order with detailed prescriptions governing social conduct, marriage, diet, and ritual purity, thereby institutionalizing a system whose roots lay in the Later Vedic age.

2.3.11 The Decline of Women's Status

One of the most consequential and deeply regressive social changes of the Later Vedic period was the systematic decline in the social, religious, and economic position of women. Compared with the relatively open and participatory environment of the Early Vedic age, Later Vedic society increasingly subjected women to restrictions that reshaped gender relations in enduring ways.

Exclusion from Ritual and Sacred Knowledge: Brahmana literature, which became authoritative for ritual practice, progressively limited women's participation in sacrificial rites and curtailed their access to sacred learning. The upanayana ceremony, which initiated individuals into Vedic study, came to be restricted primarily to males of the upper varnas—Brahmins, Kshatriyas, and Vaishyas—effectively excluding women from formal religious education and ritual authority.

Control of Marriage and Reproduction: Marriage practices also changed significantly. While Early Vedic women appear to have enjoyed greater freedom

2.3. THE LATER VEDIC PERIOD: EXPANSION, URBANIZATION, AND RIGIDIFICATION

in choosing partners, Later Vedic norms increasingly favored arranged marriages controlled by male heads of households. Evidence points to the early emergence of child marriage, with girls being betrothed or married at younger ages. The practice of svayaṃvara, in which women could choose their husbands, continued among elite families but became progressively constrained by social and familial control.

Property Rights and Economic Autonomy: As land ownership and inheritance became central to economic life, women's rights to property diminished. Wealth and land were transmitted primarily through male lines, and women had limited independent claims to resources. Their economic security became increasingly dependent on male relatives—first fathers, then husbands, and later sons—marking a significant erosion of women's financial autonomy.

The Emergence of Sati: The Later Vedic and early post-Vedic periods also saw the beginnings of the practice of sati, the ritual burning of widows on their husbands' funeral pyres. Although not universal at this stage, the emergence of this custom reflects growing notions that a woman's identity and worth were inseparable from her husband's life. This practice would persist in various regions for centuries before being formally abolished in the nineteenth century.

Spiritual and Intellectual Marginalization: Finally, women's intellectual and spiritual status declined. The female seers (ṛṣikās) celebrated in the Rigveda disappear from Later Vedic literature. In later philosophical texts, women appear more often as seekers of knowledge rather than recognized authorities. This shift reflects a broader tendency to portray women as spiritually and intellectually subordinate to men, further institutionalizing gender inequality.

Together, these developments indicate that the Later Vedic period laid the foundations for enduring patriarchal structures in Indian society, replacing earlier relative flexibility with increasingly rigid norms governing women's roles and rights.

2.3.12 The Evolution of Religious Thought: Ritual and Philosophy

The Later Vedic period witnessed a profound transformation in religious life, marked by the simultaneous intensification of ritual practice and the emergence of reflective philosophical thought. In contrast to the relatively simple domestic rites of the Early Vedic age, religion in this later phase became increasingly centered on elaborate and costly sacrifices performed by professional priests for kings and wealthy patrons.

The Brāhmaṇa texts represent a crucial stage in this development. These prose works focus with meticulous precision on the correct performance of sacrifice. They provide detailed prescriptions regarding altar construction, ritual materials, sequences of actions, and the precise recitation of hymns. The underlying assumption of the Brāhmaṇas is that ritual action, when carried out flawlessly, possesses intrinsic power to shape reality itself. A correctly performed sacrifice was believed to ensure prosperity, victory, fertility, and cosmic stability, while ritual error could nullify benefits or even invite misfortune.

This ritualistic worldview reached its most visible expression in the great state ceremonies of Later Vedic kingship—such as the Aśvamedha, Rājasūya, and Vājapeya. These large-scale sacrifices required enormous resources and served as public demonstrations of royal authority. The dependence of kings on Brahmin specialists for the performance of such rites greatly enhanced Brahmin prestige and consolidated their social dominance. In turn, Brahmins received wealth, gifts, and social privilege, establishing a durable alliance between ritual authority and political power that would become a defining feature of classical Hindu civilization.

Alongside this growing ritualism, however, developed a powerful philosophical countercurrent embodied in the Upanishads. These texts redirected religious attention from external sacrifice to internal realization and spiritual knowledge. They explore the nature of ultimate reality (Brahman), the individual self (Ātman), and the means of attaining liberation (mokṣa). The celebrated dictum "Tat Tvam Asi" ("Thou art That") expresses the core Upanishadic insight that the individual soul is fundamentally identical with the universal reality. This represented a radical departure from earlier ritual-centered religiosity and laid the foundations for Indian philosophical traditions.

The Upanishads thus mark a crucial shift in religious consciousness—from outward sacrificial action toward inward contemplation, from ritual efficacy to metaphysical understanding, and from the pursuit of material and social rewards to the quest for liberation from the cycle of rebirth. Although many Upanishadic texts were compiled in the Later Vedic or early post-Vedic period, their conceptual roots lie firmly within the evolving intellectual climate of the Later Vedic age.

2.4 Economic Development: The Evolution of Monetary Systems

2.4.1 From Cattle to Commodity Money

The economic history of the Vedic age reflects a gradual but profound transformation in systems of exchange, closely tied to wider changes in subsistence, settlement, and social organization. What began as an overwhelmingly pastoral economy, in which cattle functioned as the primary form of wealth, slowly incorporated additional commodities that operated as media of exchange and stores of value.

The Pastoral Stage: Cattle as Currency In the Early Vedic world, cattle

2.4. ECONOMIC DEVELOPMENT: THE EVOLUTION OF MONETARY SYSTEMS

constituted the most fundamental and universally recognized form of wealth. Their centrality shaped not only economic transactions but also social prestige, ritual life, and even the language of prosperity. In a society that was largely nomadic or semi-nomadic, livestock represented mobile, reproductive, and highly visible wealth, ideally suited to pastoral patterns of life and exchange.

The Agricultural Stage: The Emergence of Commodity Money As Later Vedic society moved toward settled agriculture and more complex trade networks, the limitations of cattle as the sole medium of exchange became increasingly apparent. While livestock remained symbolically important, new forms of commodity money emerged to meet the needs of expanding markets and long-distance trade.

Among the most significant of these were cowrie shells (Cypraea moneta). These shells possessed several properties that made them particularly suitable as money: they were durable, easily portable, naturally standardized in size, and difficult to counterfeit. Their adoption appears to have accelerated during the Later Vedic period as commercial activity expanded and the need for divisible, transportable currency increased. The Maldive Islands became the principal source of high-quality cowries, and specialized maritime trade networks developed to distribute them throughout the subcontinent, underscoring the degree to which cowrie currency became integrated into Later Vedic and subsequent economic systems.

Textiles and Leather as Stores of Value Alongside cowries, cotton and silk textiles functioned as commodity money in many contexts. Cloth embodied accumulated labor and skill, could be stored without rapid deterioration, was divisible into portions of varying value, and was easily transported. For similar reasons, leather and goat-skins were also used as recognized stores of value and media of exchange in certain regions, reflecting the increasing diversification of economic instruments during the Later Vedic period.

Gold in Elite Exchange Gold ornaments continued to circulate as valuable goods, especially in elite and royal transactions and religious offerings. Gold's durability, scarcity, and intrinsic appeal ensured its status as a prestigious store of value, even though it did not yet function as a widely circulating everyday currency in the way cowrie shells eventually would.

Together, these developments illustrate how the Vedic economy evolved from a predominantly cattle-based system into a more complex and diversified monetary environment, laying the foundations for later coinage and formal monetary institutions in early historic India.

2.4.2 The Significance of Monetary Evolution

The gradual transition from cattle-based wealth to commodity forms of money was not merely a technical change in the means of exchange; it was a reflection of deep structural shifts in Vedic society and economy. As communities moved away from predominantly pastoral lifeways toward settled agriculture, the practical limitations of cattle as the sole medium of exchange became increasingly evident. Herds were difficult to transport over long distances, cumbersome to divide for small transactions, and impractical within growing villages and emerging towns. The rise of permanent settlements and early urban centers therefore created a need for more portable, divisible, and standardized forms of value.

At the same time, the expansion of regional and interregional trade networks demanded exchange media that could move easily across long distances and be readily accepted by diverse communities. Commodity currencies such as cowrie shells, textiles, leather, and precious metals fulfilled these requirements more effectively than livestock. Their adoption facilitated commercial interaction between distant regions, encouraged market-based exchange, and supported the increasing circulation of goods beyond local barter systems.

Equally important was the growth of occupational specialization. As artisans, traders, priests, and administrators came to rely on regular exchange for their livelihoods rather than direct food production, the need for commonly recognized and standardized media of value intensified. Commodity money provided a practical solution, enabling the valuation of labor, goods, and services within a more complex economic environment.

In this way, each stage in the evolution of money responded directly to changing economic realities. The movement from cattle to commodity-based exchange laid the foundation for later metallic coinage and formal monetary systems, marking a critical step in the long-term development of Indian economic life.

2.5 Conclusion: Legacy and Transition

The Vedic Age represents a formative epoch in Indian history during which the foundations of Hindu civilization were laid. Over these centuries, society underwent far-reaching transformations in its social organization, religious life, and economic practices. The relatively flexible, pastoral, and tribally organized world of the Early Vedic period gradually evolved into the more complex and hierarchical order of the Later Vedic age, in which the varna system increasingly became the central framework through which social roles and status were understood.

Religious life also changed profoundly. Early household and tribal rituals expanded into elaborate, priest-dominated sacrificial systems that emphasized precise ritual performance and the authority of Brahmin specialists. At the same time, the Upanishadic tradition introduced a reflective philosophical current that sought ultimate truth through knowledge of the self and the cosmos rather than through external ritual alone. This dual development—intensifying ritualism alongside emerging philosophical inquiry—gave Vedic religion a distinctive depth and diversity that would shape later Hindu thought.

2.5. CONCLUSION: LEGACY AND TRANSITION

Economically, the period witnessed a decisive shift from pastoralism toward agriculture, accompanied by the spread of settled village life, the rise of early urban centers, and the expansion of internal and long-distance trade. The adoption of iron technology facilitated territorial expansion, supported population growth, and encouraged new forms of economic specialization, even if its impact was more gradual and complex than once assumed.

By the close of the Later Vedic period, Indian society stood at the threshold of a new historical phase. The tribal confederacies and early kingdoms of the Vedic age would soon give way to larger and more centralized states. Yet the intellectual, religious, and social patterns established during the Vedic centuries—enshrined in sacred literature, social institutions, and philosophical traditions—continued to exert a lasting influence. In this sense, the Vedic Age did not merely precede later Indian civilization; it decisively shaped its enduring character and values.

Chapter 3

Age of Buddha

3.1 Historical Context & Chronology

The centuries surrounding the life of Gautama Buddha—mark one of the most dynamic phases in early Indian history. By this time, northern India had moved decisively beyond the tribal and semi-tribal structures of the Vedic world into a landscape dominated by large, territorially defined states. These were known as the Mahājanapadas, literally "great territories of peoples." Sixteen such polities are listed in early sources, representing powerful monarchies and republican confederacies that had grown out of the older janapada system of the Later Vedic period. Their emergence reflects the maturation of settled agriculture, expanding trade, and increasingly centralized political authority.

Our understanding of this age is enriched in an exceptional way by Buddhist literature. The Tripiṭaka—the "Three Baskets" of Buddhist scripture—offers more than religious teaching; it preserves vivid details of everyday life. The Vinaya Piṭaka records rules governing monastic communities, indirectly illuminating social norms and legal ideas. The Sutta Piṭaka, containing the discourses attributed to the Buddha, frequently situates moral and philosophical instruction within recognizable social settings. The Abhidhamma Piṭaka develops systematic philosophical analysis. Particularly valuable are the Jātaka tales, narratives recounting the previous births of the Buddha. Though composed primarily for ethical and didactic purposes, these stories provide rich incidental evidence about occupations, patterns of trade, family relations, and the material conditions of life in the Mahājanapada age.

Within this complex and rapidly changing world lived Siddhārtha Gautama, later revered as the Buddha. His teaching career unfolded amid growing urban centers, intensified commercial activity, and increasingly stratified societies. Buddhism arose not in isolation but as a direct response to the moral, social, and spiritual tensions of this transforming age, and it would go on to exert a deep and lasting influence on the intellectual and cultural history of India and much of Asia.

3.2 The Mahajanapadas: Political Organization and Territorial States

3.2.1 The Sixteen Great Kingdoms

The transition from the Vedic world to the Age of the Buddha produced a fundamentally new political landscape. The loosely organized tribal confederacies of earlier times were gradually replaced by large, territorially defined states known as the Mahājanapadas. These "great janapadas" became the dominant units of political power across northern India, reflecting deeper processes of agricultural expansion, urban growth, and administrative consolidation.

Buddhist sources provide the clearest and most widely cited lists of these states. The Aṅguttara Nikāya and other texts of the Pali Canon enumerate sixteen principal Mahājanapadas: Magadha, Kosala, Vatsa (Vamsa), Avanti, Kuru, Pañchāla, Matsya (Machcha), Śūrasena, Dakṣiṇa Pañchāla, Aśmaka, Kamboja, Gandhāra, Kāśi, Malla, the Vrijjian (Vajji) confederacy, and Chedi. Together, these polities covered a vast stretch of the subcontinent, from the northwestern regions of Gandhāra and Kamboja to the eastern Gangetic plains dominated by Magadha, and from the Himalayan foothills to the Deccan fringe represented by Aśmaka.

It is important to note that no single, absolutely fixed list of Mahājanapadas exists. Other important Buddhist texts such as the Dīgha Nikāya mention only twelve major states, while Jain works like the Bhagavatī Sūtra offer alternative enumerations. These variations reflect the fluid political realities of the period: kingdoms rose, declined, merged, or were conquered, and the boundaries of power were constantly shifting. They also reflect sectarian perspectives—Buddhist texts tended to emphasize regions where Buddhism was active, while Jain sources highlighted areas of Jain influence.

Together, these sources show that the Mahājanapadas were not merely geographic entities but dynamic political formations, marking a decisive step in the evolution of Indian political life from tribal organization toward stable territorial states.

3.2.2 Monarchies and Republics: Two Paths of Organization

One of the most striking features of the Mahājanapada age was the coexistence of two distinct forms of political organization—monarchies and republics. This diversity marks a significant departure from earlier Vedic political patterns and reveals the experimental character of state formation in this period.

Several of the Mahājanapadas developed into hereditary monarchies, where political authority was concentrated in a single ruler and succession generally passed within royal families. Magadha, Kosala, Avanti, and Matsya are prominent examples of such kingdoms. In these states, kings exercised centralized control over territory, military forces, taxation, and judicial authority. The growing complexity of administration and warfare encouraged stronger central leadership, enabling monarchies to mobilize resources and armies more efficiently.

Alongside these kingdoms existed a number of republican or oligarchic states, collectively described as gaṇasaṅghas—literally "assemblies of equals." Among the most important were the Licchavis, Śākyas, Mallas, Kurus, and Pañchālas. In these polities, power did not rest with a single monarch but with assemblies composed of clan heads or leading families. Decisions regarding war, peace, justice, and diplomacy were taken collectively, and executive authority was exercised through councils and elected or appointed officials.

Buddhist literature displays notable sympathy for these republican systems, a tendency that may be connected with the Buddha's own origin in the Śākya clan, which was itself organized as a republic. The Jātaka tales and other Buddhist narratives portray both monarchies and republics as legitimate forms of governance, each possessing distinct advantages and limitations. Over time, however, the monarchies—particularly Magadha—proved more capable of concentrating military power, imposing regular taxation, and expanding territorially. As a result, many of the republican states gradually lost their independence and were absorbed into larger monarchical kingdoms.

The coexistence of these two political models illustrates the dynamic and experimental nature of political life in the Age of the Buddha, a period in which the foundations of later imperial structures were actively taking shape.

3.3 Agricultural Economy and Rural Organization

3.3.1 The Foundation: Agriculture and Village Life

The economic strength of the Mahājanapadas rested overwhelmingly on agriculture. By the time of the Buddha, the long transition that had begun in the Later Vedic age—from predominantly pastoral lifeways to settled farming—had reached full maturity. Rural production formed the backbone of state power, supplying food for growing populations, generating surplus for trade, and providing the fiscal base for administration and warfare. Buddhist sources, especially the Jātaka tales, preserve vivid descriptions of this agrarian world: ploughing and tilling the fields, sowing seed, tending crops through the seasons, harvesting, and threshing grain to separate it from the chaff.

Significant improvements in irrigation further strengthened agricultural productivity. The construction of canals, tanks, ponds, and reservoirs made cultivation more reliable, reducing dependence on erratic rainfall. Regions with access to such water-management systems could sustain denser populations and produce consistent surpluses. Nowhere was this transformation more evident than in the Gangetic plains, whose rich alluvial soils supported intensive cultivation and became the demographic and political heartland of the Mahājanapada world.

A wide range of crops underpinned this agrarian economy. Rice dominated in the wetter eastern tracts, while wheat and barley remained important in drier regions. Pulses such as lentils and chickpeas enriched the diet and restored soil fertility, and millets continued to be cultivated in marginal zones. The growing importance of sugarcane points to increasing diversification of agricultural production. Together, these crops generated the surpluses that sustained urban centers, financed state structures, and underwrote the military and administrative power of the Mahājanapada kingdoms.

In this way, village-based agriculture was not merely a subsistence activity but the central economic engine of the Age of the Buddha, shaping patterns of settlement, taxation, trade, and political authority across northern India.

3.3.2 Village Organization and Social Hierarchy

At the heart of the Mahājanapada economy stood the village, the fundamental unit of rural life and agricultural production. A typical village comprised several hundred inhabitants who collectively cultivated the surrounding fields. Each village was headed by a chief known as the grāmaṇi—literally the "leader of the village." The grāmaṇi functioned as the principal intermediary between the local community and the wider apparatus of the state. While the kingdoms levied taxes and asserted political authority, villages retained a notable degree of autonomy. They managed internal affairs, resolved minor disputes, and coordinated collective tasks such as the maintenance of irrigation channels, embankments, and reservoirs, as well as organizing communal labor during sowing and harvest seasons.

Within these villages existed a clearly defined social hierarchy. At the top were the gṛhapatis (householders or landowning peasants), who controlled cultivated plots and formed the backbone of the agrarian economy. Beneath them were the landless laborers—referred to in Pali sources as kassakas and in Sanskrit texts as dāsas and karmakaras—who worked on the lands of others and were remunerated primarily in grain or other agricultural produce. At the lowest level were slaves, who might be hereditary, captured in warfare, or reduced to bondage through debt. These individuals were compelled to labor without independent economic rights, reflecting an increasingly formalized stratification of rural society as state structures grew more complex.

The Jātaka tales, though composed for moral and religious instruction, offer strikingly realistic depictions of this rural world. They speak of ploughmen, harvesters, basket-weavers, and other agricultural specialists; they recount disputes over field boundaries, tensions surrounding irrigation and water rights, and the anxieties associated with uncertain harvests. Through these narratives, a vivid picture emerges of a society in which most people lived and worked in villages, their daily rhythms governed by the agricultural calendar and their fortunes inseparably tied to the productivity of the land.

3.3.3 Taxation and Revenue: Formalization of State Extraction

With the consolidation of the Mahājanapada kingdoms came the need for regular and dependable sources of revenue. This requirement led to the gradual formalization of taxation as a central feature of state administration. Instead of relying on irregular tribute or voluntary gifts, rulers established standardized norms for extracting a fixed share of agricultural surplus from village communities. Most literary and historical references indicate that one-sixth of the harvest was regarded as the ideal rate of taxation, though in practice this could vary— sometimes falling to one-eighth or one-tenth depending on region, crop type, and prevailing conditions.

The collection of taxes was entrusted to specialized officials. Administrators such as the samāhartā were responsible for assessing produce, collecting dues from villages, and ensuring that revenue reached the royal treasury. Over time, increasingly elaborate procedures developed to prevent both under-collection, which deprived the state of income, and over-collection, which could impoverish cultivators and undermine agricultural productivity. Later administrative literature, most notably the Arthaśāstra attributed to Kauṭilya, reflects and systematizes these practices. It emphasizes that taxation should be proportionate to a cultivator's capacity, should not damage productive potential, and should allow peasants to retain enough surplus to sustain their families and reinvest in their fields. In this conception, taxation was ideally balanced against the protection, infrastructure, and stability provided by the state.

Agriculture remained the principal source of revenue, but it was not the only one. As trade and urban life expanded, states also derived income from customs duties on goods in transit, tolls on bridges, ferries, and highways, and urban taxes imposed on merchants and artisans in towns. These non-agricultural sources grew steadily in importance, reflecting the increasing commercialization and urbanization of the Mahājanapada economy and further strengthening the fiscal foundations of early Indian states.

3.4 Trade, Commerce, and Market Development

3.4.1 Domestic Trade and Market Networks

The sustained agricultural surplus generated within the Mahājanapadas created the economic conditions necessary for the expansion of trade and commerce. As cultivators produced more grain than was required for subsistence, mechanisms evolved to distribute this surplus beyond village boundaries. At the same time, increasing occupational specialization meant that many individuals devoted themselves entirely to crafts such as pottery, weaving, and metalworking, relying on exchange rather than direct agricultural production for their livelihood. This interdependence between farmers and artisans encouraged the steady growth of internal trade networks.

Markets developed as regularized spaces for exchange in towns and larger villages. Buddhist and Jain texts provide concrete descriptions of these marketplaces. The Jātaka tales, in particular, portray bustling market scenes populated by grain dealers, spice sellers, cloth merchants, potters, and numerous other vendors. They also refer to organized market gatherings, often described as samitis, which were held at fixed places and times. These markets were subject to regulation: dishonest weights and measures could be penalized, traders might be fined for conducting business outside authorized market spaces, and in some cases the prices of essential goods were supervised to prevent exploitation of consumers.

The maturity of commercial life is further reflected in linguistic sources. The grammarian Pāṇini records a rich vocabulary connected with trade and commerce. His references to vāṇiks (merchants), śreṣṭhins and śeṣpis (specialized traders), and other commercial categories indicate that trade had become sufficiently structured and socially prominent to require systematic representation in the classical language of the period.

Together, these sources reveal a vibrant internal economy in which markets, merchants, and regulatory norms formed an essential part of daily life, laying the foundations for the even more extensive commercial networks of the early historic age.

3.4.2 Coinage and Monetary Evolution

Among the most consequential economic innovations of the Mahājanapada age was the appearance of a true coinage system. Earlier forms of exchange had relied largely on barter and commodity money—cattle, cowrie shells, textiles, and other goods—but the growth of trade, urban markets, and long-distance commercial networks created a demand for a more efficient and standardized medium of exchange. This need was met by the introduction of punch-marked coins, which represent the earliest known coinage in India.

These coins were typically made of silver, though copper examples are also known. Production involved cutting metal into roughly standardized pieces and then stamping them with one or more symbols using individual punches. Each punch impressed a distinct mark, so a single coin often carried multiple symbols. These markings served to certify weight and value and may also have indicated the authority that issued the coin. Distinct regional types—such as the Taxila–Gandhāra, Kosala, Avanti, and Magadhan series—reflect political diversity, even as the basic technology of coin manufacture remained consistent across the Mahājanapadas.

Gradually, standard weights and denominations were established. A typical silver punch-marked coin weighed about 32 rattis (approximately fifty-two grains), though some variation existed, especially in early phases. Despite their irregular shapes and hand-stamped appearance, these coins show a striking degree of uniformity, implying centralized supervision and regulation. Later administrative literature, notably the Arthaśāstra, describes systems of standardized weights and measures and emphasizes state responsibility in maintaining monetary standards, preventing debasement, and safeguarding commercial trust.

The introduction of coinage transformed commercial life. It greatly facilitated long-distance trade by allowing merchants to carry compact, widely accepted stores of value rather than bulky barter goods. Over time, coins became deeply embedded in market transactions, especially in towns and trading centers, and increasingly replaced barter for commercial exchange. In this way, the spread of punch-marked coinage marks a decisive step in the monetization of the Indian economy during the Age of the Buddha.

3.4.3 Long-Distance Trade Networks

Beyond the circulation of goods within individual kingdoms, the Mahājanapada age witnessed the steady expansion of long-distance trade networks that linked the Gangetic heartland with distant regions by both land and sea. Buddhist literature preserves some of the earliest Indian references to overseas commerce. The Jātaka tales speak of sea voyages from inland centers such as Vārāṇasī to Suvaṇṇabhūmi, a term associated with regions of Southeast Asia, including parts of present-day Myanmar and Thailand. These narratives, though framed within moral storytelling, indicate that maritime trade routes were sufficiently established to sustain organized ocean travel and commercial exchange.

Additional perspective is provided by Greek accounts from the early Mauryan period, especially the writings of Megasthenes, the ambassador of Seleucus I to the court of Chandragupta Maurya. Although his work Indica belongs to the slightly later imperial age, the trade practices he describes clearly developed from Mahājanapada foundations. Megasthenes remarks on the scale of Indian commerce, the international demand for Indian textiles and spices, and the existence of well-established trade routes and professional merchant communities. His testimony confirms that India was already an important participant in interregional trade networks extending beyond the subcontinent.

Within northern India, the Ganges River system functioned as the principal commercial artery. River transport was far more efficient than overland carriage, allowing bulk commodities—especially grain—to be moved cheaply and in large quantities. Trading towns and early cities flourished along the Ganges and its tributaries, strategically located to exploit riverine commerce. Textual references to nāvika (ship-builders and boatmen) point to the emergence of specialized occupations dedicated to constructing and operating vessels for both riverine and maritime trade, underscoring the growing technical and commercial sophistication of the age.

Taken together, these sources reveal an economy that was no longer confined to local exchange but increasingly integrated into regional and intercontinental networks, laying the groundwork for the expansive trade systems of the Mauryan and post-Mauryan worlds.

3.5 Urbanization: The Rise of Cities

3.5.1 The Urban Wave

A new wave of urban growth transformed the landscape of northern India. Fresh cities emerged, while older settlements expanded into major centers of administration, trade, craft production, and learning.

Among the most prominent urban centers were Rājagṛha (modern Rajgir), the early capital of Magadha; Pāṭaliputra (Patna), which would later become the imperial capital under the Mauryas; Vārāṇasī (Benares), the flourishing capital of Kāśi; Ayodhyā of Kosala; Śrāvastī, an important urban and religious center; Mithilā, the capital of Videha; and Ujjayinī (Ujjain), the principal city of Avanti. These cities formed a dense network across the Gangetic plains and adjoining regions, serving as hubs of political authority and economic exchange.

Although they lacked the monumental architecture of later imperial capitals, Mahājanapada cities represented substantial concentrations of population and wealth. Archaeological excavations at sites such as Hastināpura and Kauśāmbī reveal well-defined occupational layers from this period, including evidence of laid-out streets, specialized craft workshops, storage structures for grain, and signs of vigorous commercial activity. Distinctive pottery styles found across multiple sites demonstrate that goods, technologies, and cultural practices circulated widely between urban centers, pointing to the existence of established intercity networks.

This urban resurgence was therefore not merely demographic growth but a qualitative transformation—signaling the re-emergence of complex urban life in India after a long rural interlude, and laying the foundations for the imperial cities of the Mauryan age.

3.5. URBANIZATION: THE RISE OF CITIES

3.5.2 Urban Occupations and Craft Specialization

Urban centers of the Mahājanapada age provided a social and economic environment in which occupational specialization expanded dramatically. In contrast to rural villages—where most households combined farming with a limited range of supplementary crafts—cities supported dense concentrations of full-time specialists whose livelihoods depended entirely on production and exchange rather than on direct cultivation of the land. Buddhist sources, particularly the Jātaka tales, offer unusually rich glimpses into this urban occupational world.

Among the most prominent specialists were ivory workers (dantakāras), who fashioned ornate carvings and luxury goods from elephant ivory, a highly valued material traded across long distances. Weavers produced textiles of varying grades, from coarse everyday cloth to fine fabrics sought by elites and merchants. Metalworkers, skilled in iron, copper, and other metals, manufactured tools, weapons, utensils, and decorative objects. Potters supplied ceramic vessels for domestic use, storage, and commercial exchange. Carpenters and woodworkers produced furniture, carts, boats, and building components. Leather workers (chammakāras) processed hides into shoes, armor, straps, and containers, while jewelers crafted ornaments from precious metals and gemstones. Other urban specialists included tanners, dyers, perfumers, brewers, fishmongers, and numerous additional tradespeople.

The concentration of such diverse occupations fostered a sophisticated division of labor. Urban artisans relied on grain merchants for food, on potters for containers, on leather workers for tools and equipment, and on metalworkers for implements—creating a dense web of economic interdependence. Exchange was increasingly mediated by coinage and credit arrangements, allowing specialization to function smoothly. As a result, cities became not merely population centers but hubs of organized production, commercial exchange, and social complexity, marking a decisive step in the economic maturation of early historic India.

3.5.3 Urban Administration and Regulation

The growth of cities during the Mahājanapada age necessitated administrative structures distinct from those of rural villages. As urban populations expanded and commercial activity intensified, rulers developed specialized offices to maintain order, regulate markets, and manage civic life. Buddhist narrative sources, particularly the Jātaka tales, make repeated reference to officials entrusted with these urban responsibilities, indicating that city administration had become a recognizable and organized feature of political life.

Among the most important were market superintendents, described as adhikaraṇa-adhikāris, who supervised marketplaces, regulated trade practices, and ensured that weights, measures, and prices conformed to accepted norms. Police officials or commanders (daṇḍanāyakas) were responsible for maintaining public order, preventing crime, and enforcing royal authority within urban areas. In addition, municipal officers (nagara-adhikāris) oversaw civic functions such as the maintenance of streets, management of water supplies, supervision of public buildings, and general urban sanitation.

Later administrative treatises, most notably the Arthaśāstra, provide a more systematic and detailed picture of urban governance. Although compiled in the Mauryan age, this text almost certainly codifies practices that had developed gradually during the Mahājanapada period. It describes a chief city officer charged with a wide range of duties: maintaining streets and drains, organizing water supply, registering inhabitants, collecting urban taxes, regulating markets, and supervising public works. The existence of such elaborate prescriptions suggests that by the close of the Mahājanapada era, urban administration had already achieved a high degree of institutional sophistication, laying the groundwork for the bureaucratic systems of the Mauryan Empire.

3.6 Social Structure and the Varna System

3.6.1 Occupational Specialization and Jati Formation

The Mahājanapada period was a crucial transitional phase in the long evolution of India's social structure. While the fully rigid caste hierarchy of later Hindu society had not yet taken final shape, the social processes that would eventually produce it were already well under way. As economic life became more complex and occupational specialization deepened, hereditary association with particular occupations grew increasingly common. Over time, these occupational lineages laid the foundations for what would later be formalized as jātis, or caste groups.

Buddhist sources, especially the Jātaka tales, preserve valuable evidence of this development. They frequently describe families and communities identified with specific crafts and professions—leather workers, weavers, metalworkers, merchants, and others—indicating that occupations were no longer merely individual choices but increasingly embedded in lineage and community identity. Although social mobility was not entirely absent, sons were now commonly expected to follow their fathers' professions, and occupational knowledge was transmitted within families.

Significantly, early Buddhist literature, while philosophically critical of rigid social hierarchy and emphasizing moral equality, nonetheless recognizes these occupational groupings as established features of everyday life. This pragmatic acknowledgment suggests that by the time of the Buddha, such divisions were already visible and socially meaningful, even if they had not yet been fully codified into the rigid, birth-based caste system of later centuries.

Thus, the Mahājanapada age represents a formative stage in the transformation of flexible occupational roles into increasingly hereditary social groups—a development that would profoundly shape Indian society in the centuries to come.

3.6.2 The Varna System: Refinement During the Mahajanapada Period

During the Mahājanapada age, the broad outlines of the varna system became more clearly articulated, even though the extreme rigidity of later centuries had not yet fully crystallized. Social status was increasingly linked to inherited identity, but considerable flexibility in occupation still remained, especially among the upper varnas.

The Brahmins continued to enjoy the highest prestige. Their mastery of Vedic learning, ritual procedures, and philosophical knowledge made them indispensable to kings and wealthy patrons. They served as ritual specialists, royal advisers, teachers, and custodians of sacred tradition. The Dasabrahmana Jātaka portrays Brahmins engaged in diverse activities—farming, trade, and teaching—yet retaining their Brahmin identity and superior social standing. This illustrates both the adaptability and the enduring authority of the Brahmin varna during this transitional phase, even before later orthodoxy fixed Brahmins more narrowly into ritual roles.

The Kṣatriyas, associated with warfare and governance, remained the dominant political elite. Jātaka narratives abound with Kṣatriya kings and heroic warriors, reflecting their continued control over political power. In republican polities, prominent Kṣatriya families dominated assemblies, while in monarchies Kṣatriya rulers exercised supreme authority. The Buddhist tradition's emphasis on the Buddha's birth in the Śākya clan—a Kṣatriya lineage—further underlines the social prestige attached to this varna in the period.

The Vaiśyas—comprising farmers, merchants, and artisans—formed the productive backbone of the economy. As trade and craft production expanded, Vaiśya identity became increasingly associated with wealth and influence. The Jātaka tales frequently depict affluent merchants as socially respected and politically influential figures within urban society, indicating that commercial success was translating into enhanced social standing.

The Śūdras occupied a subordinate position, generally including landless rural laborers and unskilled urban workers. They were excluded from certain religious privileges, most notably the sacred thread initiation that marked formal entry into the Vedic ritual world. Even so, differentiation existed within this group: a skilled craft worker might command greater respect than an impoverished agricultural laborer.

Outside the varna framework stood groups often later termed "untouchables." These communities engaged in occupations considered ritually polluting, such as handling corpses, leatherworking, and waste removal. Evidence suggests that such groups already existed during the Mahājanapada period, although the extreme social exclusion and rigid segregation that would later characterize their status became more pronounced in subsequent centuries.

Taken together, these patterns show that the Mahājanapada era represented a crucial stage in the refinement of varna distinctions—moving steadily toward hereditary hierarchy, yet still retaining a measure of occupational and social flexibility.

3.6.3 Women and Social Status

The Mahājanapada age continued the trajectory of female subordination that had intensified in the Later Vedic period. Women were increasingly excluded from formal religious learning, denied access to Vedic study, and placed under the authority of male guardians in matters of marriage, property, and inheritance. Social norms emphasized domesticity and dependence, and public religious and intellectual life became overwhelmingly male domains.

At the same time, however, this period also witnessed the emergence of new spiritual alternatives through the rise of Buddhism and Jainism. The Buddha's decision to establish an order of Buddhist nuns—the Bhikkhunī Saṅgha—marked a significant departure from orthodox Vedic practice. For the first time, women were institutionally recognized as capable of pursuing spiritual discipline and liberation. Within the monastic framework, nuns could study, practice, and strive for enlightenment in ways that were otherwise closed to women in mainstream Brahmanical society, even though they remained subject to specific disciplinary rules and hierarchical constraints.

The Jātaka tales further illuminate women's social realities. They portray women from many walks of life—queens and princesses, merchants' wives, servants, and laborers—reflecting a society in which women's roles were generally circumscribed by marriage and household responsibilities. Yet within these narratives, glimpses of female agency, intelligence, and skill do appear. Some stories describe women engaged in trade or craft production, suggesting that while such roles were not typical, women could and did participate in economic life under certain circumstances.

Thus, the Mahājanapada period presents a complex picture: on the one hand, the deepening of patriarchal norms inherited from the Later Vedic age, and on the other, the opening of new spiritual and limited social spaces for women through the alternative religious movements that would profoundly reshape Indian civilization.

3.7 Administration and Governance

3.7.1 The Monarchy: Centralized Authority

In the monarchical Mahājanapadas, most notably Magadha, political power was organized around a strongly centralized kingship. The rāja stood at the apex of authority, exercising supreme control over administration, the military, and the

3.7. ADMINISTRATION AND GOVERNANCE

judicial system. Kingship was generally hereditary, passing from father to son, although in cases of crisis or dynastic disruption a successor might be chosen from among eligible royal kin.

Supporting the king was a structured hierarchy of officials. The uparāja (crown prince or viceroy) acted as deputy to the king and was often entrusted with regional administration or military responsibilities. The amatyas served as ministers and senior advisers, assisting in policy-making and daily governance. Military affairs were overseen by the senāpati, while financial administration rested with the bhāṇḍāgāra-adhikāri, the official in charge of the royal treasury.

Together, these officers constituted an evolving administrative apparatus responsible for managing the expanding functions of the state. Their duties included the collection of taxes, organization of the army, supervision of public order, adjudication of disputes, oversight of state enterprises such as mines, and representation of royal authority in local jurisdictions. Later administrative literature, particularly the Arthaśāstra, reflects the increasing sophistication of these systems. It outlines detailed procedures for the appointment, monitoring, and rotation of officials, aiming to prevent corruption and ensure administrative efficiency. Although such prescriptions were codified in the Mauryan period, they likely formalized practices that had been developing gradually during the Mahājanapada age.

This centralized model of governance enabled monarchies like Magadha to mobilize resources, maintain standing armies, and expand territorially—capabilities that would eventually allow them to dominate and absorb many of their republican and rival monarchical neighbors.

3.7.2 Republican Governance: Assemblies and Collective Rule

Alongside powerful monarchies, a distinctive republican tradition flourished among several Mahājanapadas. These states, known as gaṇa–saṅghas, were governed not by hereditary kingship but by collective assemblies composed of leading members of dominant clans—typically Kṣatriya household heads and aristocratic lineage leaders.

Political authority in these republics was vested in the samiti or gaṇa (assembly). The assembly functioned as the sovereign body of the state. It deliberated and decided upon all major matters: declarations of war and peace, alliances, taxation, public works, and important judicial and administrative policies. Decisions were taken collectively, and the legitimacy of governance derived from assembly consensus rather than from divine kingship or dynastic succession.

Within this collective framework, executive officers still existed. A rāja might be elected or selected from among the assembly members to act as chief executive for a fixed term, often one year or for a limited number of years. He was assisted by an uparāja and other functionaries who oversaw military, financial, and judicial functions. Crucially, however, these officials were accountable to the assembly. Their authority was delegated, not inherent, and could be withdrawn or redefined by collective decision.

In practice, republican governance was oligarchic rather than democratic. Political participation was restricted to aristocratic Kṣatriya lineages; common farmers, artisans, merchants, laborers, women, and enslaved persons were excluded from political voice. Nonetheless, within the ruling elite, deliberation, persuasion, and consensus played genuine roles. Buddhist sources preserve descriptions of extended debates and factional negotiations, especially among the Licchavis of Vaiśālī and the Śākyas of Kapilavastu, indicating that governance involved real political process rather than mere ceremonial consultation.

The conservative and consensus-based character of these assemblies made republican states relatively stable but also slow to adapt. Policy change required prolonged deliberation, and mobilization of resources could be less efficient than in centralized monarchies. Over time, this structural rigidity became a strategic disadvantage. Highly centralized monarchies—above all Magadha—proved better able to maintain standing armies, collect revenue systematically, and conduct sustained territorial expansion. Consequently, many republican Mahājanapadas were gradually absorbed into expanding monarchical empires, marking the decline of this distinctive republican tradition in ancient India.

3.7.3 Magadha: The Rising Power

Among all the Mahājanapadas, Magadha rose most decisively toward imperial dominance. Its ascent was not accidental but the result of a convergence of geography, resources, administration, and exceptionally capable leadership.

Geographic and Economic Advantages

Magadha lay in the eastern Gangetic plain (modern Bihar), one of the most fertile regions of the subcontinent. Annual alluvial deposits from the Ganges and its tributaries produced exceptionally high agricultural yields, ensuring a stable and abundant tax base. This surplus supported a large population, a standing army, and an expanding bureaucracy.

Equally important was Magadha's control over iron ore deposits, particularly in the regions of south Bihar and the Chotanagpur plateau. Iron gave Magadha access to superior weapons and tools, strengthening both military capacity and agricultural productivity. The Ganges River, flowing through Magadhan territory, functioned as a strategic commercial artery, enabling efficient movement of troops, grain, and trade goods, and integrating Magadha into long-distance trade networks extending eastward toward Bengal and overseas routes.

These structural advantages created the material foundation for Magadha's expansion.

Bimbisāra: Architect of Magadhan Power

3.7. ADMINISTRATION AND GOVERNANCE

The true architect of Magadha's rise was King Bimbisāra of the Haryanka dynasty. He pursued a calculated policy combining conquest, diplomacy, and internal consolidation.

His most important military achievement was the annexation of Anga, a prosperous eastern kingdom controlling the port-city of Champa. This conquest secured Magadha's access to eastern trade routes linking the Ganges basin with Bengal and Southeast Asia, greatly enriching the royal treasury.

Bimbisāra also used dynastic diplomacy. His marriage alliance with Kosala brought with it territorial concessions (including the strategically vital region of Kāśī), neutralized a major rival, and expanded Magadha westward. Through such marriages, Magadha steadily extended its political influence without constant warfare.

Internally, Bimbisāra strengthened administration, expanded taxation mechanisms, and maintained a well-organized army, laying the groundwork for a centralized state.

Patron of Buddhism and Jainism

Bimbisāra's reign also made Magadha a spiritual and intellectual center. He was among the earliest royal patrons of Gautama Buddha. According to Buddhist tradition, Bimbisāra met the Buddha both before and after his enlightenment and became a devoted supporter. His gift of the Venuvana (Bamboo Grove) monastery near Rājagṛha established one of the first permanent monastic centers of Buddhism. This patronage gave Buddhism royal legitimacy and accelerated its spread across the Gangetic plain.

Simultaneously, Bimbisāra supported Jain teachers, including Mahāvīra, making Magadha a major hub of heterodox religious movements that challenged Vedic ritualism.

Ajātaśatru : Consolidation and Expansion

Bimbisāra's son Ajātaśatru continued and intensified Magadha's expansionist policies. Though remembered in tradition as having imprisoned his father to seize the throne, Ajātaśatru proved to be a formidable ruler.

He fought prolonged wars with Kosala and the Vajji (Vrijjian) confederacy, weakening republican rivals and extending Magadhan authority. His campaigns demonstrated the strategic superiority of centralized monarchies over oligarchic republics.

Ajātaśatru also became a major patron of Buddhism. Buddhist tradition credits him with convening the First Buddhist Council at Rājagṛha shortly after the Buddha's death. This council systematized and preserved the Buddha's teachings, reinforcing Magadha's position as the spiritual heartland of early Buddhism.

3.8 Occupations and Labor Organization

3.8.1 The Jataka Tales as Economic Sources

The Jataka tales provide our most detailed and vivid window into the economic life and occupational organization of the Mahajanapada period. These narratives, though composed primarily for moral and religious instruction, are grounded in the everyday realities of the society in which they developed. Their settings, characters, and social interactions reflect real economic relationships, patterns of labour, and occupational structures that existed in northern India.

The Jataka tales were transmitted orally for generations before being compiled in written form and eventually incorporated into the Pali Canon of Buddhist scripture. Over time, they accumulated a vast array of descriptions of ordinary people—farmers, merchants, artisans, laborers, and rulers—engaged in everyday activities. While the moral lesson of each story remains central, the background details preserve remarkably authentic glimpses of economic life.

The collection contains more than 547 individual stories, many of which include references to occupations, production activities, market transactions, and social relations between different professional groups. We find descriptions of merchants planning long-distance journeys, craftsmen managing workshops, farmers worrying about harvests, and urban residents negotiating prices in markets. Collectively, these stories reveal a society that had moved far beyond simple subsistence living and had developed complex networks of production, exchange, and specialization.

3.8.2 Agricultural and Animal Husbandry Occupations

The Jataka tales frequently describe agricultural occupations, demonstrating that agriculture had become the dominant economic activity of the period. The most commonly mentioned figures include the kasak or hhalika (ploughman), the kassakas (cultivators and farmers), as well as harvesters, threshers, and workers engaged in irrigation and field maintenance. These occupations were not merely household activities but were clearly organized forms of labour that sustained both rural communities and urban populations.

Mention of specific crops such as rice, barley, wheat, lentils, and other pulses, reflecting regional agricultural diversity. Several stories describe anxieties surrounding crop failure, disputes over irrigation water, and conflicts regarding land boundaries. These references indicate that land ownership, water control, and agricultural productivity were critical economic concerns. Successful farming could lead to prosperity, while failed harvests could result in debt, dependence, or even enslavement.

Pastoral occupations also appear, though less prominently than in earlier Vedic literature, highlighting agriculture's increasing dominance. The Jatakas mention cowherds, shepherds, and cattle breeders who were responsible for maintaining

3.8.3 Craft and Manufacturing Occupations

The Jataka tales provide extensive evidence of a flourishing craft economy, particularly in urban centers. Crafts were no longer confined to household production but were carried out by specialized artisans who worked in workshops and supplied goods for local markets and long-distance trade.

Metalworkers and smiths appear frequently in the stories, working with iron and copper to produce agricultural tools, weapons, and household implements, as well as decorative ornaments and vessels. Their craft required technical expertise in smelting and forging, and such workers occupied respected positions in society.

Weavers and textile workers are among the most prominently mentioned occupational groups. The stories describe the processes of spinning, dyeing, and weaving, and they refer to cotton, silk, and other textiles. Cloth was a major trade commodity, and the tales often depict weavers involved in commercial exchange, producing both everyday fabrics and fine garments for elite customers.

Woodworkers and carpenters produced carts, furniture, chariots, boats, and building materials. Their work was essential for both urban infrastructure and trade activities. Similarly, potters supplied ceramic vessels for cooking, storage, and transport of goods.

Leather workers, though sometimes associated with ritual impurity, are acknowledged as indispensable producers of shoes, straps, armor, and containers. Ivory workers carved luxury objects for royal and wealthy patrons, indicating the presence of elite consumption markets.

In addition, the Jataka tales mention jewelers, dyers, perfumers, painters, sculptors, and other specialists, revealing a remarkably diverse and well-developed manufacturing economy.

3.8.4 Trade and Commercial Occupations

The Jataka tales preserve rich descriptions of trade and merchant activity. Merchants appear as major social and economic actors who organized caravans, financed voyages, and conducted both inland and overseas trade. The stories refer to land routes across the Gangetic plains as well as sea voyages to distant regions such as Suvarnabhumi in Southeast Asia.

Merchants, shopkeepers, moneylenders, and traders operated in regulated markets, where officials supervised trade, ensured proper weights and measures, and imposed penalties for fraud. Marketplaces are depicted as vibrant centers of economic life where goods ranging from grain and cloth to jewelry and perfumes were exchanged.

These narratives reveal the emergence of a monetized economy, supported by the circulation of punch-marked silver coins. The ability to accumulate wealth through commerce allowed merchants to become influential patrons of religious institutions, including monasteries and charitable establishments.

3.8.5 Labor and Servitude

The Jataka tales clearly acknowledge the presence of wage laborers and slaves as integral parts of the Mahajanapada economy. References to kammakaras (paid workers) and dasas (slaves or bonded servants) appear in a wide variety of social and occupational settings, indicating that labor was no longer confined solely to family-based agricultural work but had become an organized and market-dependent activity.

Several tales describe laborers employed on farms, in workshops, and in merchant households. These narratives frequently highlight the difficult conditions under which wage workers lived—their dependence on daily wages, their vulnerability during times of crop failure or economic downturn, and their exposure to harsh treatment by employers. At the same time, some stories portray compassionate masters who recognize the hardships of their workers, revealing that labor relations were not uniformly exploitative but varied widely according to circumstance and individual character.

Slavery is also depicted in a nuanced manner. Slaves appear as domestic servants, agricultural laborers, and assistants in commercial establishments. Unlike Brahmanical legal texts that would rigidly define servile status as hereditary and socially fixed, the Jataka tales present slavery more as a social condition shaped by debt, misfortune, warfare, or personal circumstances rather than as an immutable identity. Individuals might move into or out of servitude over the course of their lives, and the narratives frequently emphasize moral conduct rather than birth status when evaluating a person's worth.

This relatively pragmatic and fluid treatment of labor and servitude reflects the broader intellectual climate of the age. Both Buddhism and Jainism, which emerged during this period, challenged the rigid hierarchical assumptions of Brahmanical orthodoxy and emphasized ethical behavior, compassion, and the moral equality of human beings. The Jataka tales, rooted in these traditions, therefore preserve an economic and social vision in which servitude existed as a real and often harsh condition, yet one that was not metaphysically fixed and could be altered through circumstance, conduct, and social change.

3.9 Currency and Monetary Systems

3.9.1 Evolution from Commodity to Coined Money

The economic development of the Mahajanapada period was accompanied by a decisive transformation in systems of exchange. While barter and various forms of commodity money—such as cattle, textiles, and cowrie shells—continued to function in everyday transactions, the growing scale and complexity of trade demanded a more efficient medium of exchange. It was within this context that coinage emerged as one of the most important economic innovations of the age. The introduction of punch-marked coins provided a standardized, portable, and divisible form of money that was far better suited to expanding commercial networks than earlier systems of barter or commodity exchange.

The earliest punch-marked coins were relatively simple and somewhat crude in appearance. They were often irregular in shape and bore a limited number of punch symbols, primarily serving to indicate the weight of the metal and, by implication, the authority responsible for issuing them. These early coins were essentially functional tools of exchange rather than carefully finished objects, reflecting an experimental phase in monetary practice. Over time, however, coin production became increasingly refined. The number and style of symbols became more standardized, weight regulations were enforced more carefully, and the association between particular symbols and specific issuing authorities grew clearer. As a result, merchants and consumers gradually developed confidence in the reliability of coinage. A trader encountering a coin bearing familiar symbols could reasonably estimate its value, trust its metal content, and recognize the political authority that guaranteed its legitimacy.

The establishment of standardized weight—commonly around 32 rattis (approximately 52 grains)—was particularly significant. It allowed merchants to calculate prices and payments with far greater precision than had been possible under barter systems or with loosely defined commodity currencies. Large and complex transactions could now be conducted through the exchange of coins rather than through cumbersome negotiations involving grain, livestock, or other bulky goods. This change was especially advantageous for long-distance trade. Merchants traveling across regions could carry their wealth in compact metallic form, greatly reducing the risks, costs, and logistical difficulties associated with transporting physical commodities. In this way, coined money not only simplified everyday exchange but also actively promoted the expansion of regional and interregional commerce, laying the foundation for more integrated economic networks across northern India during the Mahajanapada age.

3.9.2 Regional Coin Types

As coinage became firmly established, different Mahajanapadas began issuing coins with distinctive regional features. These variations made it possible for merchants, officials, and consumers to recognize not only the metal content and weight of a coin but also the political authority that guaranteed its value. In effect, each major kingdom developed a recognizable "monetary signature," and these regional types together formed an interconnected monetary landscape across northern India.

Among the most prominent were the Taxila–Gandhara type, associated with the northwestern regions; the Kosala type, issued in the powerful kingdom of Kosala; the Avanti type, from the central Indian kingdom of Avanti; and the Magadhan type, which originated in Magadha and would eventually become the most influential. Each of these types bore distinctive combinations of punched symbols. Magadhan coins, for example, frequently carried symbols associated with royal authority as well as marks linked to merchants or merchant guilds, suggesting a close relationship between political power and commercial activity.

Over time, as kingdoms expanded through conquest and as trade routes linked distant regions, coins of different types began to circulate together within the same markets. A merchant in one city might handle coins issued by several different Mahajanapadas, each with its own symbols and weight conventions. This created increasingly complex monetary environments in which traders needed to understand not only the intrinsic metal value of coins but also the customary exchange rates between different regional issues. The coexistence of multiple coin types thus reflects both the political fragmentation of the period and the growing integration of its commercial networks, revealing a dynamic and evolving monetary economy at work across the Mahajanapada world.

3.9.3 State Control and Standardization

The growing use of coinage also reflects the increasing involvement of the state in regulating economic life. Coin production was not left entirely to private initiative; rather, it became an area in which political authorities gradually asserted oversight and control. Although Kautilya's Arthashastra belongs to the later Mauryan period, the systems it describes almost certainly developed from practices that were already taking shape during the Mahajanapada age. There existed conception of the state as the ultimate guarantor of monetary reliability and commercial fairness.

According to the Arthashastra, the state maintained strict standards for the weight and purity of coins, regulated the scales and measures used in markets, and imposed penalties for fraudulent practices such as clipping coins, producing counterfeit currency, or manipulating weights. Such measures were designed to protect both state revenue and public confidence in the monetary system. A reliable coinage was essential not only for facilitating trade but also for ensuring that taxes, fines, and other state revenues could be collected fairly and predictably.

The remarkable consistency seen in surviving punch-marked coins—despite their hand-stamped and individually produced nature—strongly suggests that some form of standardization was already being enforced during or even before the Mahajanapada period. The uniformity of weight ranges, the repetition of recognized symbols, and the relative purity of the metal used all point to deliberate regulatory practices rather than random or purely private production. These early efforts at monetary standardization laid the groundwork for the more centralized and formalized fiscal systems that would later be perfected under the Mauryan Empire, marking an important stage in the institutional development of the Indian state.

3.10 Credit, Lending, and Financial Instruments

3.10.1 Emergence of Credit Systems

As trade networks widened and agricultural production generated regular surpluses, economic life during the Mahajanapada period began to depend increasingly on organized systems of credit. Commerce could no longer function solely on immediate exchange; merchants, farmers, and craftsmen often required capital in advance, and this need was met by the growing class of banias—merchant-moneylenders who combined trading activities with financial services.

These banias acted both as suppliers of goods and as creditors. When a merchant wished to organize a trading expedition, particularly one involving long-distance or maritime travel, he frequently required funds in advance to purchase goods, hire labor, and arrange transport. Similarly, cultivators might seek loans to survive the interval between sowing and harvest, to recover from crop failure, or to meet tax obligations. In such circumstances, moneylenders provided loans, typically charging interest that reflected both the time involved and the perceived risk of non-repayment.

The Jataka tales contain repeated references to borrowing, lending, repayment, and indebtedness, indicating that these practices were not exceptional but had become routine features of economic life. Debtors, creditors, and disputes over unpaid loans appear naturally within the narratives, suggesting that the audience was already familiar with such arrangements and their consequences. These literary allusions reveal a society in which credit had become an established financial instrument—one that supported commercial expansion, smoothed seasonal fluctuations in agricultural income, and bound individuals into increasingly complex economic relationships

3.10.2 Interest and Debt Relationships

References in both literary and legal traditions indicate that loans during the Mahajanapada period were commonly issued at interest, reflecting an increasingly sophisticated understanding of money as capital capable of generating profit over time. Interest rates are described in various sources and, when converted into approximate modern equivalents, generally appear to have ranged between

12 and 24 percent annually, though these rates were not uniform. They could vary widely depending on the nature of the loan, the length of time involved, the borrower's reputation, and the perceived risk to the lender. A merchant embarking on a hazardous long-distance trade journey, for example, might be charged a higher rate than a cultivator borrowing to manage seasonal expenses.

The Jataka tales contain numerous episodes that revolve around borrowing, repayment, and the tensions created by debt. Some stories describe honest debtors struggling to meet their obligations due to misfortune, crop failure, or commercial loss, while others portray unscrupulous lenders exploiting the vulnerability of borrowers. These narratives reveal that although credit was essential for facilitating trade and smoothing economic life, it also carried the potential for serious social consequences.

In certain cases, inability to repay loans could lead to severe hardship. Some Jataka stories describe individuals who, overwhelmed by debt, were forced into forms of servitude or bonded labor in order to discharge their obligations. This suggests that debt could, under particular circumstances, result in the loss of personal freedom, effectively transforming economic dependence into social subordination. Such portrayals underscore both the benefits and dangers of expanding credit systems—while they supported economic growth and opportunity, they also introduced new forms of vulnerability and inequality into Mahajanapada society.

ChatGPT can make mistakes.

3.10.3 Guild Credit and Mutual Aid

Alongside individual moneylenders, the emerging guild system played a vital role in shaping the financial life of the Mahajanapada period. Guilds were not merely professional associations of craftspeople and merchants; they also functioned as important financial institutions. Within these organized bodies, members could obtain credit to support their commercial ventures, whether to purchase raw materials, expand workshops, or finance trading expeditions. By pooling resources and collective trust, guilds reduced the individual risks faced by their members and made larger-scale economic activity possible.

Guilds also facilitated transactions through their shared reputation. A merchant belonging to a well-known guild enjoyed greater credibility in the marketplace, making it easier to secure loans, enter into contracts, and negotiate favorable terms. In effect, guild membership served as a guarantee of reliability and professional conduct, much like a modern business association or credit rating. This collective reputation helped stabilize commercial relations and encouraged broader participation in trade.

In addition to their financial functions, guilds often acted as internal courts for resolving disputes among members. Commercial disagreements over debts, contracts, or quality of goods could be settled within the guild, reducing the need for intervention by royal authorities. Through such mechanisms, guilds provided a form of mutual aid—supporting members in times of need, facilitating access to credit, and offering institutional protection. These practices reveal that economic cooperation had become highly organized, and that collective financial security was already an important feature of urban commercial life during the Mahajanapada age.

3.11 The Rise of Magadha and Political Consolidation

3.11.1 Military and Administrative Innovations

The gradual rise of Magadha as the most powerful Mahajanapada was not accidental; it was the result of a combination of favorable geography, strong economic foundations, and deliberate political and military innovation. Situated in the fertile eastern Gangetic plains, Magadha possessed abundant agricultural resources that generated substantial tax revenues. Control over important riverine and land trade routes further strengthened its economic base. These advantages allowed its rulers to experiment with and sustain administrative and military reforms that were beyond the capacity of many rival states.

One of Magadha's most significant innovations was the development of a standing army—a permanently maintained force rather than a temporary militia assembled only during times of conflict. This represented a major departure from older tribal and semi-feudal military systems. Maintaining such a force required steady financial resources, regular provisioning, and an organized administrative structure to oversee recruitment, training, and logistics. Magadha's ability to support a standing army demonstrates both the efficiency of its revenue system and the centralized authority of its rulers. A permanent military establishment gave the kingdom greater readiness, discipline, and strategic flexibility, enabling it to respond swiftly to threats and to pursue sustained campaigns of territorial expansion.

Technological superiority further strengthened Magadha's military power. The widespread use of iron weapons, produced in the kingdom's smithies, provided a clear advantage over rivals that still relied more heavily on bronze or mixed technologies. Magadha's access to iron ore deposits and its organized capacity for large-scale metal production meant that its armies could be more consistently and uniformly equipped. Iron swords, spears, arrowheads, and armor were generally stronger and more durable than their bronze counterparts, enhancing both offensive and defensive capabilities. The ability to manufacture and distribute such equipment in quantity reflects Magadha's emerging military-industrial organization and helps explain how it steadily outmatched and absorbed neighboring states during the Mahajanapada period.

3.11.2 Strategic Expansion

Magadha's rulers did not rely solely on military strength; they pursued territorial growth through carefully planned and strategic expansion. One of the earliest and most significant examples of this policy was Bimbisara's conquest of Anga. This campaign brought a large and fertile territory under Magadhan control and, more importantly, secured the Champa River region, which served as a vital corridor for trade moving toward the eastern and southeastern parts of the subcontinent. By gaining access to these routes, Magadha strengthened its commercial networks, increased state revenue, and enhanced its strategic position in regional trade.

This expansion was not merely opportunistic but formed part of a broader pattern of consolidation. Control over Anga provided Magadha with greater access to maritime and overland trade connections, allowing its merchants to participate more actively in long-distance exchange networks. The economic benefits of this expansion further reinforced Magadha's capacity to maintain its standing army and administrative apparatus, creating a self-reinforcing cycle of power, wealth, and military capability.

Subsequent rulers continued this policy of aggressive and calculated expansion. Through a combination of warfare, diplomacy, and strategic alliances, Magadha gradually absorbed or subordinated neighboring Janapadas. Over time, this process transformed Magadha from one powerful kingdom among many into the dominant political force across much of northern India, laying the foundations for the imperial unification that would later be achieved under the Mauryan dynasty.

3.11.3 Intellectual and Spiritual Prestige

Magadha's ascendancy was reinforced not only by military strength and administrative efficiency but also by its growing intellectual and spiritual prestige. The early patronage extended to the Buddha and his teachings by Bimbisara and later by Ajatashatru gave Magadha a unique association with new currents of religious and philosophical thought that were transforming the spiritual landscape of northern India. By supporting the Buddha, providing land for monasteries, and offering protection to the Buddhist community, Magadhan rulers positioned their kingdom as a center of ethical inquiry, learning, and spiritual experimentation.

The establishment of monastic complexes such as the Venuvana near Rajgir attracted monks, scholars, and pilgrims from distant regions. These institutions became spaces for teaching, debate, and the preservation of sacred doctrine. At the same time, Magadha also supported Jainism, whose leaders and ascetics found patronage and protection within its territories. The coexistence of multiple philosophical traditions fostered an environment of intellectual vibrancy, making Magadha a crossroads of religious dialogue and scholarly exchange.

As Buddhism spread beyond Magadha into other Mahajanapadas and, later, across much of Asia, the kingdom's status as the birthplace and early patron of the Buddha conferred lasting symbolic authority. This spiritual association amplified Magadha's influence far beyond what could be achieved by military conquest alone. Its reputation as a sacred and learned land enhanced its cultural prestige, strengthened its legitimacy in the eyes of neighboring rulers and populations, and contributed significantly to its emergence as the dominant power in northern India during and after the Mahajanapada period.

3.12 Conclusion: Transformation and Legacy

The Mahajanapada era represents one of the most formative phases in Indian history. During this period, the subcontinent underwent far-reaching transformations that reshaped its political, economic, social, and spiritual foundations. Small tribal and kin-based communities gradually gave way to sixteen major territorial states, creating a new political geography dominated by organized kingdoms and republican confederacies. At the same time, advances in agriculture and irrigation supported growing populations, while expanding trade networks and the rise of urban centers fostered occupational specialization and complex economic relationships. The introduction of standardized coinage and credit systems further facilitated commerce and integrated regional economies into broader networks of exchange.

Equally significant were the spiritual and intellectual revolutions of the age. Buddhism and Jainism, which emerged during this period, introduced new ethical ideals and philosophical perspectives that challenged aspects of older Vedic traditions. Their emphasis on moral conduct, compassion, rational inquiry, and the potential for spiritual progress irrespective of varna status offered alternative pathways of thought and practice. The support these movements received from powerful rulers such as Bimbisara and Ajatashatru helped transform them from local reformist traditions into major religious currents that would leave an enduring imprint on Indian civilization and beyond.

Politically, the gradual consolidation of power—culminating in Magadha's hegemony—laid the structural groundwork for imperial unification. The administrative innovations, military organization, revenue systems, and economic networks developed during the Mahajanapada period created the institutional framework upon which the later Nanda and Mauryan dynasties would build. Although the Mahajanapada era formally concluded with the rise of the Nandas, its legacy endured. The Mauryan Empire, especially under Ashoka the Great, would draw heavily upon these earlier foundations, transforming regional kingdoms into a subcontinental empire. Thus, the Mahajanapada age stands not merely as a transitional phase, but as the crucible in which the political, economic, and spiritual contours of classical Indian civilization were decisively shaped.

References

[1] Agrawal, D.P. (1982). "The Archaeology of India."

[2] Majumdar, R.C. (1977). "Ancient India."

[3] Possehl, G.L. (2002). "The Indus Civilization: A Contemporary Perspective."

[4] Akhilesh, K. & Pappu, S. & Rajapara, H.M. & Gunnell, Y. & Shukla, A.D., Singhvi, A.K. (2018). "Early Middle Palaeolithic culture in India around 385–172 ka reframes Out of Africa models"

[5] Wong, K. (2018). "Stone Tools from India Fan Debate over Origins of Cultural Complexity."

[6] Foote, R.B. (1866). "On the Occurrence of Stone Implements in Lateritic Formations in Various Parts of the Madras and North Arcot Districts."

[7] Possehl, G.L. (1980). "Indus Civilization in Saurashtra."

[8] Trinkaus, E. (2011). "Late Pleistocene Adult Mortality Patterns and Modern Human Establishment."

[9] Egyankosh. "Origins of Agriculture and Domestication of Animals"

[10] Risch, R. & Boivin, N. & Petraglia, M. D. & Gomez-Gras, D. & Korisettar, R. & Fuller, D.Q. (2011) "The prehistoric axe factory at Sanganakallu-Kupgal (Bellary District), southern India"

[11] Paliwal, K. "Ancient Indian Metallurgy."

[12] Walimbe, S. (2022). "Protohistoric human skeletal evidence in India: Research status and prospects"

[13] Britannica. "Great Bath."

[14] Lkouniv. Kumar, Dr. A. "Copper Hoards."

[15] Dongre, Dr. N.L. "Prehistoric Copper Implements in the Gungeria-Balaghat Region."

[16] Youngintach. "Paleolithic Age: Pallavaram Handaxe and Attirampakkam Cleaver."

[17] Deccan Chronicle. "Maski: Karnataka's Small Town with 6000-year Civilisational Legacy."

[18] Zenodo. "Ancient Ingenuity: A Reappraisal of Indus Valley Town Planning."

[19] Sharma, Dr. M. (2020). "The Indus Valley civilization Urban Planning and social structures."

[20] Peepultree. "Robert Foote: Finding India's Stone Age."

[21] Gyanvigyansangam. "Urban Planning and Indus Valley Civilization."

[22] Kanika, B. (2021). "Early Indus Civilization and Its Trade Relations."

[23] GK Today. "Rig-Vedic Economy."

[24] Guarnieri, N. (2023). "Counting Cowries: Shell Money of Greater India."

[25] Vamadevananda. (2018). "The Meluhhans in Mesopotamia, Egypt and Africa."

[26} Maitra, Dr. L. (2023). "The Quaint Cowrie Trade that Linked the Maldives with Eastern India."

[27] Bhatia, P. (2007). "Mining and Metallurgy in Ancient India."

[28] Induqin. "Adichanallur: Significance Of The Iron-Age Burial Site In India's Ancient History"

[29] New Indian Express. "Adichanallur inhabitants grew paddy during Iron Age: Report"

[30] Upadhyaya, N. & Mishra, S.K. (2024). "Analysis of the Scientific Achievements of the Indus Valley Civilization."

[31] Kulke, H., & Rothermund, D. (2016). "A History of India."

[32] "Rigveda."

[33] Parpola, A. (1994). "Deciphering the Indus Script."

[34] Mittal, B. (2024). "An Analysis of Vedic Period in Terms of Physical Activities and Their Symbolism in the Rigveda Scriptures."

[35] Egyankosh. "Unit 8: Vedic Period-I."

[36] Nagalaxmi, V. (2022). "The Role and Position of Women in Vedic Period in India."

[37] Pushpam, Dr. K. N. (2024). "Status of Women in the Rig Vedic Period."

[38] "The Satapatha Brahmana."

[39] Dutt, S. (2021). "The Role of Iron Tools/Implements in the Later Vedic/PGW Culture."

References

[40] Koul, S. (2024). "A Comparative Analysis of the Four Vedas: Rigveda, Samaveda, Yajurveda, and Atharvaveda."

[41] Reddy, P. B. "Mahajanapadas - Rise of Magadha, Nandas, Invasion of Alexander."

[42] Winternitz, M. "Most Ancient Buddhist Records."

[43] Egyankosh. "Society and Economy."

[44] Bhatia, C.P. (2023). "Taxation and Tax Administration as Depicted in Ancient Indian Texts."

[45] Income Tax India. "History of Direct Taxation."

[46] Gangadharaiah, Dr. B.R. "Bimbisara and Ajatashatru: The Magadhan Kings."

[47] Mondal, R. (2018). "Lay-Life of India as reflected in Pali Jataka."

[48] Kumari, B. (2013). "Evolution and Development of Guilds in Ancient India."

[49] Tripura University. "Ancient Indian Political Thought."

[50] Saha, S. & Khatum, S. (2023). "Wisdom of the Past: Exploring Political Governance and Administration in Ancient India through Shantiparava and Sukra Niti Sara."

References

About The Author

Amrit Kumar is a researcher in Economics with a primary focus on the economic history of the Indian subcontinent, the history of economic thought, and contemporary socio-economic and geo-economic issues. His academic interests extend beyond economics into Actuarial Science and Data Science.

He can be reached at kamrits@outlook.com and can be followed on GitHub at https://github.com/AmritKumarS.

About The Author

www.ingramcontent.com/pod-product-compliance
Lightning Source LLC
Chambersburg PA
CBHW031448210526
45464CB00005B/2370